W9-CZS-359

BELIEFS
OF A
UNITED,
METHODIST
CLINTON M. CHERRY

1908 Grand Avenue
Nashville, Tennessee 37203

TO THE MANY
in all walks of life
who contributed in any way
to my thinking about
"THE ONLY WISE GOD"
to Whom
"be glory for ever more
through Jesus Christ"
(Romans 16:27)

CONTENTS

Foreward

FOREWORD

The average person is a theologian whether he knows it or not! Even those who are superstitious are saying, in effect, that they believe in a power beyond themselves which can harm them if they do or don't do certain things. This is, actually, a form or animism, a relic of primitive religion. Animism, wherever and however it is manifested, implies beliefs that are properly understood as theological. They are beliefs about the God or gods (spirits) that are supposed to influence our lives.

Almost everybody gets involved sooner or later in discussions that revolve around such expressions as: "What is to be is to be"—"It was God's will"—"What did I do to deserve this?"—"All religions are the same"—"You don't have to belong to church to be good"—"He never did anybody any harm"— "I don't believe in hell"—and so on. All of these commonly heard words are theological, in one way or another. It seems impossible to avoid saying what we believe, even when we do not really know what we are talking about!

Again, there is a universal curiosity about differences in "religion," a term frequently used of differing denominations within Christianity, particularly its Catholic or Protestant forms. This interest has actually increased since the advent of ecumenism and the gratifying openness it has encouraged. More than ever people are asking theological questions that must be answered in order to explain differing practices or varying forms of worship. This questioning extends to non-Christian faiths, for there is emerging a new appreciation of other religionists and their right to their own, if differing beliefs.

In fact, there is a new generosity of attitude toward nonbelievers, those who do not subscribe to faith in God. This, it is said, is a pluralistic society and must make room for all kinds of people. The one virtue of our day seems to be freedom, understood as individualism, and an individualism too often measured by license. There are anarchists who oppose anything organized, and nihilists who seem to be against everything that is. Yet they have the right to speak, and are protected by the laws of the society they despise. Whatever their highly individualistic attitudes, which no brief description can represent justly, all non-conformers must be adjudged with the fairness which is their due in a system that draws its strength from beliefs other than theirs. What are these beliefs? What is the faith that undergirds our constitutional democracy? It is commonly thought to be that of a "nation under God" who guarantees "liberty and justice for all." It is a theological faith.

Finally, there is "the conflict of science and religion," to use the time-worn phrase. In a day of technology, when "scientific miracles" increasingly minister to human needs and contribute to the realization of human hopes, and the scientists himself is becoming the one person who "knows it all," the question is whether there is any place for religion and its historic theology. Science seems to be looking forward, religion backward. Yet science, skilled in the "how" of things, is silent concerning the "why" in any large and comprehensive sense. It has no way with its techniques to discover the purpose of existence or the ultimate goal of life. These are theological considerations.

All this being so, it is inevitable that any one who wants to know "what life is all about" and desires to live it abundantly must have his own theological beliefs. He must be convinced for himself about God and man, existence and identity, decision and duty, death and destiny. He must have his own beliefs about his relation to others, beginning with his own family and ending only with the whole human race. He must plant his spiritual feet on the rock of faith which he has tested and found solid enough to stand on amid the storms of life. He must, in short, be a theologian.

This little book is an attempt to help the average person, the layman, to arrive at his own faith, to forge his own theology. It is not technical, does not use theological language, and is not written for professional theologians. But it does take account of theological ideas discussed by them, and of present-day currents of thought which concern them —and everyone who thinks at all. It does take its stand within that tradition of Christian emphases represented by John Wesley, Philip Otterbein, Jacob Albright—and it is addressed to the United Methodists who are today's heirs of their faith and labor in the 18th and early 19th centuries.

But it is the basic meaning of Christianity rather than a denominational expression of it that is here sought, and it is hoped that this little book will be found useful by those who may stand outside of the specific church of whose adherents it is immediately addressed.

To you who seek a meaningful Christian faith, greetings! May your seeking be rewarded with finding (Jeremiah 29:13), and may the door open for you to a richer life with God in Christ. (Luke 11:9-13)

CLINTON M. CHERRY

1

WHAT IS RELIGIOUS FAITH

There is nothing more important in life than one's faith.

Every one has a faith of some sort. Even those who say they do not believe in God believe in life (or they would not want to live), in themselves (or they would be unable to do anything), in their families (for whom they work and sacrifice, from whom they receive encouragement and inspiration), in their community and country (or they could not be good citizens), in humanity (or their usefulness would be limited to their race or class).

Faith provides the dynamic of living. It gives us something to live for. It indicates what we consider most important in life.

But what is religious faith?

The word religion means "that which binds." Religious faith is a faith that binds us to God, or what we accept as God. For all practical purposes, those who call themselves humanists make humanity their God, and so their faith in humanity is of the nature of religious faith. In communist countries, the state has become more or less deified and receives from party adherents a devotion that is all but religious. For all of us, what we have accepted as the highest value in our lives, what gives us the deepest satisfaction, what commands our greatest loyalty is really our God. It could be our job on the one hand, or our family on the other—there are many possibilities—and such a devotion is really our

7

religion. This is what Jesus suggested to the rich man who came to him asking about eternal life. Jesus discerned in him not a love for what eternal life really meant, but a love for what this life meant in terms of wealth. So he told him to sell all he had and to become a disciple. (Mark 10:21) But he did not love eternal life as represented by Jesus as much as he loved this life as represented by his wealth! His God was money.

Religious faith, then, is a faith in God as the highest loyalty in our lives. It does not shut out other faiths of a lesser sort, such as those mentioned above, but it takes precedence over them. Belief in God may exclude a lesser faith, because at times a lesser faith makes impossible a larger one. Our belief in ourselves may, for example, be a self-love that excludes the love of others. While we must have faith in ourselves, we must also believe in others, or we can not live a full life. And we must be sure that no lesser faith interferes with the supreme faith, the faith in God.

Religious faith is faith in God as the supreme value in our lives. If we have an adequate understanding of God, belief in Him takes in every other good belief and shuts out every unworthy faith. It is the test of all our faiths. Our loyalty to God will enable us to choose among our other loyalties, and enable us to decide when one takes precedence over the others. This explains Jesus' otherwise difficult saying: "If any one comes to me and does not hate his own father and mother and wife and children and brothers and sisters, yes, and even his own life, he cannot be 'my disciple." (Luke 14:26) Does Jesus mean this literally and absolutely, or figuratively and relatively? We know that he spoke in the latter way as a Jew who used concrete rather than abstract language. We know that he did not hate his parents, or his brothers and sisters, or himself. But he gave up family life for himself in view of his mission, and, though he struggled with the prospect of unwelcome death in Gethsemane (Mark 14:32-

42), he accepted it and gave himself on the cross in obedience to the will of God for his life. In his case religious faith bound him to God in a loyalty that had to take precedence over other loyalties.

We must decide what is the most important thing to us, believe in it, and be loyal to it. We must hold all other loyalties subject to it. This is religious faith. It is faith to God.

2

WHY DO WE BELIEVE IN GOD?

Why do we believe in God? There is a simple and direct answer. It makes sense to do so.

Some people think they believe in God because they can prove He exists. This is really impossible. If we could prove the fact of God, God would be the result of our logic. We should really bring God into existence by our proofs. We should be creating God! In terms of logic, God must be our basic premise. In terms of fact, God simply is. He exists before and beyond us, greater than our proofs, more than all we can think or know about Him.

To believe in God, we say to ourselves that He just is, and then find reasons why it is important to us to believe in Him. These reasons are not proofs of God's existence, but arguments we find reasonable to us. It then makes sense to us to believe in God.

Strange as it may seem to most of us, there are those to whom the belief in God does not seem to make sense. Some of these specifically reject faith in God and are atheists, A Greek word which means apart from or without God. These persons are not unbelievers. They have other beliefs of the sort mentioned in the last chapter, and they find their motives for life in those faiths which we consider inferior to faith in God. But atheists may be very fine people. They are as varied in personality as theists (believers in God), and most of them, having had a struggle to give up the tradi-

11

tional faith, are quite dedicated to the beliefs they have accepted. It is possible, without giving up our faith in God, to have much in common with atheists.

Other non-believers, as we might call them, are known as agnostics. These people find belief in God beyond them. If they could, they would believe in Him. But they cannot find the arguments they need to establish Him for themselves. And so they say that they do not know whether He is or is not. The term agnostic implies those apart from or without knowledge (of God). Many of these are devoted persons exhibiting what we might call the Christian spirit. Many greatly admire Christ. Some of them attend church. Others are pray-ers. Their prayer might well be: "Lord, if you exist, help me in my belief." (See Mark 9:24) With such seekers believers can have very much in common.

What, then, are the reasons we need for God to make sense to us? Each person will have his own reason for this justification, but let us consider several here. There is the world in which we find ourselves. It is a world we did not make, to which we owe our very existence. Here, then, is that on which we depend, here before we came, here during our stay on this earth, here after we will have gone. The creative and sustaining power the world represents we attribute to God.

But let us take a look at the larger universe of which our earth is a part. We know that it is on the move, even the stars (once thought to be "fixed") being in motion, the whole process being full of energy that links somehow with mass (substance)—and "up to something," as we say. Judging by our earth there seems to be a purpose in it all, an evolution (development) from the inanimate (non-living) to the animate (living), and, in the amazing display of the animate, a parallel development of plant and animal life interlocking in an interdependence sometimes called the "balance of nature." At the climax of it all stands the animal known as man, to whom is given the obvious privilege of making use of the whole. (Genesis 1:29,30) To the theistic mind it seems unbelievable that such a process could be accidental. It is, we feel, a creation, a "creative evolution," the work of a Mind to match our minds which appreciate it.

Let us look closer at the man who can thus understand the universe, however limitedly. It is amazing to realize that of all that exists, so far as we know, only man even knows its exists! The stars, the planets, the inanimate, the animate up to the level of man, is unaware of existence, much less the scheme of things. Man is not only aware of the universe, but can explain its operation in mathematical terms. Shall we say that mathematics does not belong to the scheme of things? Shall we not say that the universe exhibits the reality of a mathematical Mind, not in the stars, or planets, or rocks, but in the creative process that organized matter (substance) in mathematical patterns? To us who begin with the fact of God, God is established as at least a mathematical genius!

And there is the mystery of life itself. We know it is an energy of some sort. "Protoplasm," the substance within living cells, is constantly on the move. Life reproduces itself. Life develops, grows, adapts, learns variously throughout the plant or animal world. Shall we say that all this just happened—or came about according to plan—in accordance with a power built into it? To the theist, at least, the emergence of life and its development into ever more sophisticated forms, resisting all the forces that would extinguish it, speaks eloquently of God at work.

Beyond life is the mystery of personality. What does it mean to be a person? It means to be aware of oneself, to know one exists, to distinguish oneself from others, and yet to stand "outside" oneself and judge oneself, to set for oneself ideals and goals, to have a faith and to commit oneself to it. All the marvel and challenge of human life is wrapped up in the mystery of personality. Whence is it? Surely we cannot claim to have endowed ourselves with it. True, we are what we decide to be: But even this is not possible without a desire to be—and to be what we can be intense, personal terms. Whence this desire and this individualism? Shall we say that we give these capacities to ourselves? Or shall we say that somehow all that we are and hope to be we owe to the Power and the Plan at work in the universe before we came into existence, and to be at work long after we will have laid down our lives here on earth? This Power and this Plan we call God.

We believe in God because it is not enough to believe in man, who is not responsible for his own existence. It is not enough to believe in a universe which, as a thing, cannot in quality measure up to man. We believe that we must look beyond ourselves and our world to the God who accounts for all that is. Man must hope in God beyond anything man can do. (Psalm 39:7) Only so can man be fully man, in actuality and in potentiality.

But how are we to picture God? We cannot. We must know God by what He does, in the world He has made, in the life He has given, in our own experiences which reach for Him. We believe in the atom which the most powerful miscroscope cannot discern because of the atomic power which is so awesome in both threat and promise. So we believe in God, as sure of Him as of our living and breathing (Acts 17:28), and we are willing to wait until we know at last Him who may seem to us to be at times the blurred image in a tarnished mirror. (1 Cor. 13:12) We hope for the time when our present encounter with God, as if in the dark (Genesis 32:24), will be a glorious confrontation, "face to face." (1 Cor. 13:12)

3

OUR RELATION TO GOD

To believe in God is not necessarily to have dealings with God. Voltaire, the French skeptic, is reported to have said concerning God, "We bow, but we do not speak." But if it is important to believe in God, it is even more important to have a personal relationship to Him.

Here we must make a distinction between "it" and "you," the impersonal and the personal. We can know about somebody, perhaps somebody great in history like George Washington or Abraham Lincoln. We can know that these men lived and that the one was the "Father of his Country," the other its Savior. But this is a secondhand, impersonal knowledge. We know about, but are not acquainted with, either Washington or Lincoln.

On the other hand we know our relatives, our friends, in a quite personal way, and there is at least one person in our lives to whom we are committed in a relationship of personal trust.

It is such a trust in God that is the true meaning of faith. Faith in God is a person-to-person relationship.

This means that man is made for God and God is interested in man. That is a tremendous faith indeed, but it is implied in Genesis 1:27 which says that man is made in the "image" of God. This surely means that, like no other creature in creation, man is related to God in a likeness that makes possible a mutual fellowship. Here is to be found the reason

15

for man's existence, and the explanation of the remarkable development of the universe from things to life, and from life to human life, a creative evolution by which God brought forth on this earth (and perhaps elsewhere on other "earths") those whom He can call His children.

In this respect human beings are to be distinguished from the animals. We can know animal life only by inference from animal behavior, but we do not seem to detect in animals anything more than a simple acceptance of life, instinctive behavior without contemplation, and an ignorance of death as a problem. How different with human beings! We ask why we are born and what life is all about. We seek a sense of identity, and crave recognition. We are bothered with the question of right and wrong. We have notions of what is true, what is good, what is beautiful. We wonder about life after death, especially when we lose some one we dearly love. We know the meaning of love as more than lust, and more than blood relationship. We know love of honor, and of country, and of humanity—and we can die for a dream! How strangely different we are!

Above all we have a freedom that makes us both proud and anxious. We can choose to be what we want. We do not want another to take this freedom from us. Yet we are afraid, not really knowing how to use it. Our freedom is what makes us persons, aware of ourselves as individuals, and yet it threatens our security for it can cut us off from other persons. We want to be ourselves but we want also to belong to others. And we want them to belong to us.

We find also that we want to belong to God. As we think about Him, we find a hunger in our hearts for Him. As Augustine, the great theologian of the fourth century, put it in a prayer: "Thou hast made us for Thyself, and our hearts are restless until they rest in Thee." Here in this hunger for God we seem to find the meaning of being made in His image God is our Father, and we belong to Him. We want to know more than that He is; we want to know Him as He is. We want to fellowship with Him in prayer, in meditation, in just thinking about Him and what He means to us.

The counterpart to this is that God wants to fellowship with us. It is for this that He brought into being the universe, the countless stars and sun with their planets, the earth or earths where there is life and children of God such as we are. How sobering to think that God went to all this trouble to make possible the beings that bear His image! And the end is not yet. As Paul puts it: "The (whole) creation waits with eager longing for the (final) revealing of the sons of God." (Romans 8:19)

The goal of our living, then, must be to come into a living fellowship with God in a person-to-person relationship, beginning now and extending into a limitless future, if God so wills. But we must freely choose this way of life. God will not compel us. Though He has the power, as revealed in the mighty forces that operate in the universe, God will not reduce us to the status of robots, mechanical men. He has limited Himself with respect to our freedom, and what happens to us is what we choose.

It is true that there are limitations on our freedom. It is true that we are conditioned by the circumstances of our life, or the people who influence, even compel, us. It is true that physical and moral and spiritual handicaps can circumscribe our freedom very closely and narrow it to what may amount to necessity. But we are human and the children of God only to the extent that we are free, and make real choices, and prove our personhood and our responsibility by the choices we make.

Why does God want it this way? Because, being God, the Other Person, He can have fellowship only with persons. There is no personal fellowship with things. We can fellowship with God and enjoy His Presence only as we prove ourselves capable of a person-to-person relationship by the responsible use of our freedom. We can have this relationship with God only when we freely choose to be the kind of persons God wants us to be.

4

CHRISTIANITY AND OTHER RELIGIONS

God is God, and man is made of God. The way in which man has sought and found God is described by the general term religion, "that which binds" man to God. It may sound surprising to say that religion is man-made but it is true in the sense that it represents a human effort to recognize and realize the Presence of God in life. This effort has found many expressions in the story of humanity, and there are in the world today a number of living religions. Their differences of belief and of practice constitute a problem for the adherent of any one of them. Which is the "right" one? Or are all religions equally true"?

If there is one God, as we believe, how can there be many ways to Him? One answer is that religions are like the spokes of a wheel all of which end in the hub, the center of the wheel. They may begin at different points on the circumference where the wheel goes to work, but they all draw their strength and their common purpose from their central concern for God. There is truth in this conception. All religions do have a common purpose and all are true in this sense. They want to relate man to what is more than man, what will ennoble his living and give it purpose and direction. But all religions do not have the same hub of understanding (of God), nor do they together join smoothly in a continuous circumstance to do the same kind of job for humanity.

A better analogy might be that of a number of automobiles

with a varying supply of gasoline in their tanks. Depending on the amount of fuel each has, it can go only so far to the common destination. Depending also on its springs and other structural elements, each will provide a more or less smooth ride over the sometimes rocky road of life. Depending again on the power of the engine in each case, the steep slopes encountered will be negotiated with relative success or failure. But in the case of all of them, the destination is the same. Representing religions, their purpose is to reach God with their precious passengers of human beings, and so effect a final union in the Father's House. (John 14:2)

All analogies are more or less defective, and the foregoing one leaves out another vital function of religion. All religions are concerned not only with the final union with God but with present fellowship with Him and what that means for living in this world. It amounts to a foretaste of the "best that is yet to be." It may be compared with seeing pictures of an absentee relative whom one is about to meet in person, or reading letters of a friend whom one knows only by correspondence but will soon known by contact. There may be such preparation for the final meeting, much to do that will keep one quite busy, others to reach who will also be in the consummation of a happy relationship. One's whole life will be influenced and altered by the great purpose that takes command. Religion in this sense becomes a commanding way of life. (Phil. 1:27; Col. 3:2)

But in some religions, and to some extent in all religions the way of life becomes more important than the God for which it is an anticipation, even substituting for God in any personal sense. Self-discipline becomes a goal in itself. Buddhism, for example, began with the promulgation by Gautama of "four noble truths" (concerning suffering as caused by wanting too much), which yielded a "noble eightfold path" of disciplined behavior, with "Nirvana" or the feeling-less state as the highest hope of the "enlightened" (as the word *buddha* means). It is a strange irony that Gautama who ignored the gods of Hinduism was himself made by his followers into a deity of countless manifestations. In various other ways, such as Yoga in Hinduism, or mysticism in all religions, the tendency is to manipulate human activity, feelings, and thoughts, so as to produce immediate effects. The purpose is to save oneself, by one's own efforts, from the failures and frustrations of life by retreating from it into the inner sanctuary of meditation. As one cuts himself off from life, from its desires and ambitions, its feelings and hopes, its ecstasy and agony, he himself becomes less human, less personal, and God seems less necessary as the Other Person. God becomes an IT, a vast impersonal consciousness, a great ocean in which one loses his identity as a drop of water is lost in the sea.

The religion of the Bible is strikingly different. In the Bible we deal with the God who acts," who makes His name known to Moses as I AM, or, better, I WILL BE (Exodus 3:14), who reveals what he is by what he does, delivering his people from Egypt, establishing with them a covenant at Sinai, bringing them into a "Promised Land," raising up for them a kingdom through the dynasty of David, a kingdom that finally became for the apocalyptic prophets the Kingdom of God—for, all along, God was regarded as the King and the earthly ruler of the moment was but his viceroy, "the Lord's anointed" (1 Sam. 16:6, 12-13), which in Hebrew is the word "messiah." This biblical view of God is to be sharply distinguished from the ancient Gods understood in terms of nature's cyclic seasons, repetitive and without ultimate meaning (See Ecclesiastes 1:2-11)—and from the philosophic God of the ancient Greeks who saw him as the "Unmoved Mover," at the top of the heap of creation, desired but undesiring, unaffected by the toil and trouble of human life, removed from this evil world, its mistakes and sins. In contrast, the Biblical God was in the struggle, and working with his people to bring good out of evil, not only in the world but in their own lives. The Bible has no cyclic view of history but a linear, straight-line, one. History is going somewhere—with God; and where it is going is where God intends, to the ultimate society, the final (and so eternal) consummation of God's purpose, in which not the individual merely but the people as a whole, one and all, live under the Fatherly Kingship of God.

This unique view of God makes Judaism, and its outgrowth, Christianity, a unique accomplishment. Shall we say that here is found the best religion? No, not in terms of indivious comparison. But we must say that what is here is unique. There is no other religion like it. It has contacts with other religions, since all religions seek God in one form or another, but these contacts are not equivalents, least of all identities. The Judaeo-Christian faith needs to be friendly in its attitudes, since its mission is to be light where there is darkness (Isaiah 49: 6; Matt. 5:14-16), and light is a friendly thing in a dark room! But it does not need to be compromising. There is no pooling of insights if they do not see alike. There is only the sharing of insights ("This is the way I see it"). The comparing of viewpoints is, in the long run, the only way in which a true view of things can finally be obtained. Until there is a better understanding of life and of God than what we have in the Bible, we are obligated to testify to that which has come to us, by way, we believe of a genuine revelation from God.

But must Christianity be distinguished from Judaism? Yes, if we are to understand our distinctive role as Christians. Both religions root in the Bible. But the foundation of Judaism is found in Moses and the Torah seen as the Covenant of God with his chosen people, duly sanctified by sacrifice. (Exodus 24:3-8) The cultural inheritance of Judaism, typified by its *kosher* practices, and the clannishness of the Jews, stamp the religion as legalistic and ingrown. Christians have, very sinfully, been responsible for much of the defensive attitude displayed, for the Jews have suffered incalculably at Christian hands through history. Their proud conviction of being to this day in their own way a "light to the Gentiles" is to be admired. We Christians must beware "lest we) be wise in (our) own conceits" (Romans 11:25), and should feel toward the Jews a gratitude and an appreciation we have too long delayed according them.

Nevertheless, Christianity has its own justification in what God has done in history, and has its own God-given mission. Its foundation is found in Jesus Christ and his covenant of love sealed with his blood on Calvary. Our Torah is the Law of Christ found primarily in the ethics of the Sermon (Teaching) on the Mount (Matthew, chs. 5 to 7)—but it is a law of liberty (James 1:25) as based not on "the letter" but the Spirit (2 Cor. 3:6), the Spirit of God which inaugurated the church at Pentecost (Acts, ch. 2). Christians, then, do not look to the past for a legalistic justification but to the future in a dynamic faith in the still unfolding will of God, led, as we must be, by his spirit. This openness to the future is also an openness to the world (Luke 13:29). We are not, and must not be, a closed fellowship. To all this we must testify. We have no right to hide this light "under a bushel" but are obligated to let it "shine before men." (Matthew 5:15,16)

5

THE PROBLEM OF SIN

What is sin? Attitudes toward this theological concept, so prominent in the Bible, have undergone great change. People are much more tolerant in their thinking about sin, and much more critical concerning traditional notions of what sins really are. They rarely think of themselves as sinners. They are quick to find mitigating circumstances or justifying motives. Could not sin be regarded as simply a mistake, inevitable for human beings, and may not one learn from his mistakes? Or is not sin a legitimate expression of irrepressible instincts: sex, hunger, curiosity, possessiveness, belligerence, all grounded in body mechanisms? "No one is perfect," it is glibly said. One may be a good person in many ways despite his natural failings. He must be judged not by what he is not in this or that particular, but what he is in ways which make him a well-integrated person, well-adjusted to society, and helpful to others.

It must be said that such a dismissal of sin as is suggested above is not an adequate understanding of sin in the Christian sense. Sin is a theological word, not a scientific one. It can never be adequately described in scientific terms, whether medical, psychological, or sociological, though it has consequences in all these areas of life. Sin is not a physical necessity, not a mental illness as such, not just the breaking of the law. It is what may lie behind these aspects of human behavior. And its cure is not medicine of any kind.

What then is sin? It is basically a bad relationship to God and to man. It is alienation. It is the attitude of pride toward God and of selfishness toward others. Asked by a scribe (a Pharisaic expert in the Biblical Torah of Law) what the greatest commandment was, Jesus selected two as the summary of the whole number: love of God and love of one's neighbor as oneself. By this test, sin is the rejection (Romans 1:18) of God's law of love (1 Cor. Ch. 13), whether written in a code or not. (Romans 2:12)

For the Law of Love is greater than any commandment, and cannot be regulated by a set of rules, however many. Jesus felt free to set aside the sabbath rules in order to "do good on the Sabbath Day" (Mark 3:4), and he ignored ritualistic requirements as meaningless for heartfelt behavior. He went far beyond the demand of the Torah in laying down the "law" of love. (Matthew 5:38-48) Paul speaks of the "law of the Spirit of life in Christ Jesus," a law of freedom which liberates one from the "letter" (wording) of the Torah by the new covenant (II Cor. 3:6) of Christ's love. Paul himself shows independence of mere wording in his delineation of Christian love in I Corinthians 13, not once quoting Jesus' words but everywhere exhibiting his spirit. Paul knew what Jesus meant by sacrificial love. "It is no longer I who live, he testified . . . The life I now live in the flesh I live by the faith in the son of God who loved me and gave himself for me." (Galatians 2:20)

The Christian ethic of love is disciplined. It is not "lawless" in the sense that it does not matter what is done. Though neither Jesus nor Paul were slaves of the Torah, they were not against the Torah as a means of understanding God's will (Matthew 5:17; Romans 7:7), even if, as representing the Old Covenant, it did not fully represent God's intention for His children. (Matthew 5:20; Mark 10:5,6) Paul did, indeed, fall back into legalisms, perhaps because circumstances permitted nothing better and that rules and regulations are secondary to human relations inspired by Christian love. Christian love is disciplined by what can be accomplished of good for the Body of Christ, the church (I Cor. 12:12-27), and for the body of humanity where love acknowledges God as the universal Father (Ephesians 4:6), and all men as good as oneself. (Ephesians 4:2)

Now sin strikes at this ethic of love with its pride. The meaning of the sin of Adam, the primeval man, as told in Genesis Ch. 3, is that of pride which was guilty of more than disobeying a specific command of God. (Genesis 3:3) It was guilty of overreaching the limits of man's creaturehood. The same theme is found in the story of the tower of Babel. (Genesis 11:1-4) This raises the question of the limits God places upon man. Does God say to human efforts, "Thus far . . . and no farther." Does God disapprove, for example, of the fantastic ventures of current science not only into outer but also inner space, reaching out to the planets and in to the sub-atomic? No, it is not what man can do as man, what man can make of himself, that is the problem of sin. If he makes a god of himself, if he forgets his dependence on God, if he struts as God, then he is a sinner, rejecting the love of God that is expected of him. It is noteworthy that the great scientists are humble men who have great respect for "nature," and have no intention but to obey its laws. They understand quite well what a pioneer of science, Bacon, said: "Nature is only subdued by submission." There is no pride in true science.

Sin also strikes at the ethic of love with its selfishness. Selfishness has its roots in a self-centeredness that derives from infancy when one is, inevitably for the sake of his very survival, the center of parental attention. Wise parenthood will at the earliest time possible wean the child not only from his bottle but from his awareness of his own hungers to those of others, teaching him to help and to share and be a "member of the team." The effect of these early years persists into later life. But one's demand upon others for his own needs should grow into the recognition of mutuality, the need of every one for everybody in a life where we can not go it alone. This is the basis of human love, which is more than instinctive. It depends on recognition and acceptance as the way of living.

Yet self remains in the picture, as Jesus suggested. Everybody must be somebody. The basic problem of existence is identity. One is bound to ask, "Who am I" What am I worth? What can I do?" If one cannot accept himself and find for himself a place among people, getting the recognition that this requires, then he is in trouble with himself. If one despairs of himself and perhaps hates himself for what he is not, then he is in trouble with others. He projects his hate, by psychological inversion, as a hate of others, and punishes himself by punishing others. These extremes of attitude may need to be treated by a phychiatrist, but in the end a moral decision is necessary. When he has "come to himself" (Luke 15:17), the one who has not understood himself must realize that his selfcenteredness is a sinful attitude to be renounced and replaced by a love of others based on a love of self. The Golden Rule comes into play in all directions: one resolves to wish for others what he wishes for himself, and wish for himself what he wishes for others—and all wish for all that which contributes to the good of all. This attitude of mutual good will is the meaning of Christian love on the human level.

What role does conscience have in all this? Conscience is a word that, strangely, does not appear in the Old Testament of the Bible. It derives from Stoicism, a popular moral philosophy in the Graeco-Roman world, and the Greek word suggested self-knowledge in the sense of self-judgment. It is closely related to the basic meaning of personality which, as we have seen, is self-awareness, consciousness of self, but in the sense of the kind of person one is. One of the great capacities of our humanity is the ability to criticize self, and in this is the promise of what we may be beyond what we are.

Yet conscience in itself does not know right from wrong! Conscience, then, needs education. It needs to be given the knowledge necessary to make choices. (Herein lies the importance of parental training and the education of our growing youth.) It is possible to regiment conscience by the restriction of knowledge to only one side of any issue with the result that conscience can know no better and must approve only a one-sided view. This explains the variation of behavior between sections of a country, or between countries and cultures with their differing traditions of right and wrong.

We are made aware of sin through our consciences (Romans 2:15-16, but, since our consciences can grow in understanding, we can have a developing feeling about what is right or wrong. Thus Saul could "in all good conscience" persecute the church (Acts 23:1)', though the later Paul could be bothered by his conscience as the "least of the apostles (I Cor. 15:9) for having done so! We must live lives of openness to God's leading that we might "grow in the grace and knowledge" of God. (II Peter 3:18)

Is sin to be distinguished from temptation? We think of sin as a deed (stealing, killing) or a word (lying, slandering) but it is also a thought since it springs from pride or selfishness. Jesus was interested in the teaching on the Mount to drive it back to its source in the heart and mind, and so he finds murder to be hate (Matt. 5:21-26), adultery to be lust (5:27-28), foreswearing to be duplicity (5:33-37), retaliation to be lovelessness. (5:38-48) But when is a thought or feeling a sin? When is it not more than a temptation? The simple answer must be that a temptation which is rejected is no sin, as in the case of Jesus himself who turned aside the blandishments of the devil with convictions concerning his personal commitments to God. (Matt. 4:1-11) But when a temptation is accepted as a plan of word or action, it is already a sin, even though yet but a thought, as in the case of Judas whose desperate scheme to betray Jesus into the hands of his enemies, with such tragic consequences, was so entrenched in self-centered thinking that he could not but eventually carry it out. (Mark 14:18-21)

Sin is really a terrible thing, whether of thought, word, or deed. It is disruptive of loving relationships, destructive of the best in life, disrespectful of God who is the source of our being, the Hope of all we may be. It needs to be guarded against the portals of our minds and exercised from our innermost thoughts and desires. It is the unloving attitude in a world where, because God made it, "love is the law of life." (Kagawa)

6

THE EXPERIENCE OF SALVATION

Sin is alienation, separating man from God and man from man. It provides no realization for the individual himself, as the Prodigal Son of Jesus' parable discovered (Luke 15:14-16). It results in the break-down of human institutions (marriage and the home, communal life at any level), making for a sick society. The punishment of sin is not so much the meting out of specific penalties for specific sins (though specific sins do at times have specific results) as the inevitable consequences that follow a breakdown of the good relations which God intends. In the moral order which is an aspect of creation, God "gives us up," to borrow a phrase of Paul, to what follows as the result of alienation (Rom 1:24,26,28).

Salvation is an intensely personal matter, for it has to do with the reconstruction of one's attitude. We "come to ourselves" (Luke 15:17), we arise and go to our heavenly Father" (v. 20), we confess our sin and our unworthiness (v. 18; cf. Psalm 38:18), we "humble ourselves under the mighty hand of God" (I Peter 5:6). This calls for the renouncing of pride and self-centeredness, and it is not easy to do. But we must do it. Only we can do it. God cannot save us in spite of ourselves, nor can any one else.

In this reconstruction we find special meaning in the cross of Christ. We read in Acts that when Peter at Pentecost charged the people with crucifying and killing Jesus who was none other than Lord and Christ (Acts 2:23,36), they

31

were "cut to the heart" and cried, "What shall we do" (2:37)?
Luke also records that those who returned from Calvary beat
their breasts. In his account the centurion, who ordered the
Luke also records that those who returned from Calvary beat
man was innocent" which implied that the centurion felt
guilty about it. Certainly, one of the results, and therefore
one of the purposes, of the cross was to show how sinful
sin really is: it crucifies the Son of God! As somebody put it,
"Every time we sin, we drive the nails deeper into the hands
and feet of Christ." If the cross will not reduce us to that
humility we need in order to see sin as it is and foreswear
our pride which spawns it, is there anything else that will?

The second stage in the experience of salvation is that of
divine forgiveness. Why can we not forgive ourselves, and be
done with it? There is a sense in which we must. There are
those who never forgive themselves, who have an abnormal
desire to punish themselves for ever. This is an emotional
disorder which needs psychiatric treatment before the Christian experience of forgiveness is really possible. We must be
able to accept forgiveness, if forgiven, whether by God or
man. We cannot help to restore a broken relationship by
extending a closed fist. We must put out an open hand. We
must be willing to receive what is given us.

And forgiveness is a gift. Jesus makes it a mutual gift in
the triangular relationship we must have in life: to God, to
others, and to self. We pray for forgiveness because we are
willing to forgive. (Matt. 6:12) Jesus makes clear that we
can not be forgiven unless we forgive. (6:14-15) But Luke's
version of the Lord's Prayer, expanded in a parable of Jesus,
puts the emphasis on the generosity of God (Luke 11:1-13),
comparing him with the normal human father. The understanding of forgiveness inheres in our human experiences, but
forgiveness cannot be complete as only a human realization.
God cannot be left out of the three-way relationship whose
circle is broken. Reconciliation between man and man, and

no more, is not a complete reconciliation. In fact, it is not a thorough-going one unless it originates with God. God is the Father of all men, as we have seen, and we are reconciled to our brother before God, as Jesus pointed out. (Matt. 5:23,24) Unless we are reconciled with him as a child of God, we are not reconciled. Sin is extremely subtle. (Genesis 3:1) We must be sure that we recognize its character. It is there, "crouching at our door" ready to overpower our best-intentioned impulses. The only way to overcome the sinful self is to look away from it to the God in whom self and others find their tri-unity with him.

God must therefore be the author of forgiveness. In the Old Testament God is pictured as "merciful and gracious, slow to anger, and abounding in steadfast love and faithfulness . . . forgiving iniquity and transgression and sin, but who will by no means clear the guilty. . . " (Exodus 34:6-7) The Mosaic Torah provided a complex system of sacrifices, among them sin and guilt offerings, but none for sins "with a high hand" (i.e., deliberate sins) for which the sinner must be cut off from his people. (Numbers 9:13; 15:30) Sacrifices were to be made and among the most important were those effecting atonement, or fellowship with God, both animal (Leviticus 17:11) and vegetable (Lev. 5:11-13), but also, surprisingly, non-sacrificial offerings. (Exodus 30:15) It was not the offering but the spirit that mattered (Genesis 4:6-7), and it was God who provided atonement on the basis of the spirit manifested. The sacrifices were simply various means by which God and his people got together. But it was God who bore sacrificially with his sinful people (Hosea 11:8-9), not the people who placated an angry God.

It is this basic understanding of God, already evident in the Old Testament, that becomes clear in the Cross of Christ. "God was in Christ," Paul wrote, "reconciling the world to himself, not counting their trespasses." (II Cor. 5:19) How did Paul know this? From his own experience of Christ, "the

Son of God who loved me," as he put it, "and gave himself for me." (Gal. 2:20) Here is the second meaning of the Cross: not just the measure of our sin but also the proof of God's immeasurable love for us. Here the atonement God provides does not even wait for worthiness on our part. "For our sake" God makes "him sin who knew no sin, so that in him we might become the righteousness of God." (II Cor. 5:21) This means that Jesus who was condemned by the Torah as a sinner because he was hung "on a tree" (Galatians 3:13—Deutreronomy 21:23) was the means by which God set aside the sacrificial system of Moses and broke through with his "unmerited grace." The earliest experience of this grace of God in the Christian sense was the experience of Pentecost when the disciples, though they forsook Jesus and fled (Mark 14:50), were nevertheless for Jesus' sake forgiven and accepted for the kingdom of God. It was this new conviction on their part which enabled Peter to proclaim at Pentecost: "Repent . . . and you shall receive the gift of the Holy Spirit." (Acts 2:38)

It is through Christ that we experience salvation. We see him as God's gift of forgiveness and reconciliation. We find ourselves bound to God and to every man. "He is our peace" who has broken down dividing walls of hostility" (Ephesians 2:14) to "reconcile us (all, regardless of our former alienations) to God in one body through the Cross" (2:16)— and to what end? That we may be "rooted and grounded in love . . . the love of Christ which surpasses knowledge, that we may be filled with all the fullness of God." (3:17,19)

This is the experience of salvation. It is regrettable that is has been regarded as anything else but a person-to-person reconciliation based on love. But it has been referred to as a "transaction," as if it was a deal—and it has suffered from the metaphors applied to it, some of them deriving from Christian history. The intention has been sincere: to make our "election sure." (II Peter 1:10 But salvation is not basically a bargain with the devil, or a satisfaction of the divine honor, or the outweighing of sin in the scales of justice, or the substituting of one victim for another. These are man-made theories of the atonement, trying to explain how God goes about forgiving us. We do not need to.

We are called to believe that God will and does forgive us, and to take him at his word in Christ. We are called to accept that forgiveness, and let God's love fill our lives to the full and overflow into the lives of others. (Romans 5:5) We are invited to find in our own experience, not in speculation about God, that salvation is a glorious reality!

For us who are United Methodists it is a privilege to remember that salvation as an experience has been central to our faith from the beginning. For all his philosophy and logic, John Wesley had no peace until he "felt (he) did trust, in Christ alone for salvation," and in that trust received "an assurance" that "he had taken away (his) sins, and saved (him) from the law of sin and death." The emphasis on experience which made Wesley a "Methodist" was reflected in the preachers and converts in America of both the English and German traditions, a common experience that makes them now properly one fellowship.

It is this experience that is the United Methodist witness to the meaning of Christianity. It is this experience that can be, with prayers and confident expectation, the happy poss-session of every Christian seeker of any "name or sign."

7

THE LIFE OF THE SPIRIT

In the last chapter we saw that the disciples' experience of salvation through Christ was at the same time the gift of God's Spirit. Much the same thing is implied in the testimony of John Wesley concerning the assurance given him that Christ had taken away his sins and saved him from the law of sin and death. This is an echo of Romans 8:2. But Wesley was also thinking of Romans 8:16 which speaks of the "witness of the Spirit" which assures us that we are children of God. For Wesley as for the disciples at Pentecost, salvation was an experience of God's Spirit. And it was not the only experience. Wesley taught the possibility of entire sanctification, an experience of "perfect love" when one would be so filled with the Holy Spirit he would lose all desire for sin, though he might still be subject to the frailties and failures of human life. He would, however, be fixed in love upon God and his will. It was this conviction that gave John Wesley his distinctive doctrine of Christian perfection (Matt. 5:48), framed for his preachers in the questions asked when they are received into conference membership: "Are you going on to perfection?"—Do you expect to be made perfect in love in this life?"

But what is the Holy Spirit by which, indeed, all of us go from grace to grace (John 1:16) and be changed into "the likeness of the Lord" from "one degree of glory to another"? (2 Cor. 3:18) Is it some *thing* other than God himself? Is it a power, an impersonal energy like steam or electricity, or even the wind that fills the sails of boats or windmills? How are we to understand the description of Pentecost (Acts, ch. 2) which speaks of "a sound . . . like the rush of a mighty wind? and of "tongues as of fire"? The qualifying words "like" and "as" indicate that the Spirit is not a wind or a fire, not a power in the impersonal sense. The Spirit is God in action!

All our religious language is analogical. We speak of God himself in spacial terms. He is "above" or "within" or "the ground of our being," but we know he is not "up" or "in" or "under." These analogies are not descriptions but comparisons with experiences we have which give us a certain feeling that we can associate with God. The Bible is very careful not to give a picture of God. Revelation, ch. 4, records a vision of God seated on his throne in heaven, but will say no more of him than this: "He who sat there appeared *like* jasper and carnelian." (4:3) Exodus 33:20 says flatly that God cannot be seen, and John 1:18 confirms this with the words, "No one has ever seen God." By the time of Christ, God was so far removed from human experience in the feeling of the people that his name (probably Yahweh) was never pronounced (the phrase "the Lord" being substituted for it), and even the word "God" was replaced by other words having equivalent meaning: "Blessed" (Mark 14:61)— or "Power" (Mark 14:62; cf. Acts 7:56) or "Heaven" (as in Matthew which regularly says "Kingdom of Heaven" instead of "Kingdom of God"). God's name was the unspoken name above every name. (Philippians 2:9)

There was need, therefore, for an intermediary means to connect God with man. In the story of Creation, Genesis records simply "God said, 'Let there be' . . . and there was." But in time the "word" of God came to have a special meaning as God's agent, and the later Aramaic translations of the Hebrew used the phrase, "The Word (Memra) of God," as in Gen. 3:9 where the Aramaic says, "The (Word of) the

Lord called to Adam," the bracketed words not being in the Hebrew. Isaiah 55:10-11 describes the independent power of God's Word as if it were another Being. In the same way the word "Wisdom" was made a personal agent of God, as in Proverbs, ch. 8, for anything God would say or do would be a product of his Wisdom. In the Fourth Gospel the personalized "Word of God" incarnates ("becomes flesh") in the human Jesus (1:14), for the work of salvation (1:12-13). In Revelation 19:13, Christ is the Word of God in judgment. God therefore operates through the Word in creation, in salvation, and in the consummation of his purpose. This use makes the Word God's means of reaching the world of men. (John 1:9-13)

In the same way the Holy Spirit must be understood as the means by which God is at work in special activities. In the Old Testament any unusual endowment was refererd (in accordance with the understanding of the day) to the power of God's Spirit. (Genesis 41:38; Judges 14:6; 1 Samuel 11:6; 16:13) It was by this power that the prophets could speak, declaring the Word of the Lord saying "Thus says the Lord" (as at Amos 1:3,6,9,11,13; 2:1,4,6—a series of striking "oracles"). The Holy Spirit, "poured out" at Pentecost, was understood as the prophetic word. (Acts 2:17-18) The disciples, previously timid, now bold in their witness (Acts 4:31), conscious that God was speaking through them since they were "filled with the Holy Spirit". (4:8; 13:9) They had to "obey God rather than men" (5:29) because they had to witness, in cooperation with the Holy Spirit, to what God was doing. (5:32)

To put all this into our own language, the life of the Spirit is simply life with God, having a sense of his presence, influenced by his will, dedicated to his purpose, sustained by the consciousness of his help in whatever we do for him. We are not to think that God pours into us what we do not know as one might pour water into a tumbler—the Spirit is not a liquid! But the presence of God in our thoughts and prayers does give an insight others do not have, and an assurance of truth not to be discovered by "worldly wisdom." (cf. 1 Cor. 2:6) We have the "mind of Christ" (2:16) whose obedience even unto the cross (Phil. 2:8) might seem foolish, if not scandalous (1 Cor. 1:23), to the worldly wise, but to those who are informed with the Holy Spirit, is the very wisdom and power of God.

This influence of God upon us extends to all aspects of our being, if we let God's Spirit have his way with our lives. We may not have thought of it, but it is possible to be but partially saved. A complete salvation is when God has captured all the area of our life. We must begin, of course, with the knowledge of God's love given and our sins forgiven, but we must translate this wonderful conversion-experience into the complete transformation of every area of our life. God's grace toward us must not be in vain. (1 Cor. 15:10) And it is God's Spirit which completes the good work begun—and only begun—in us with our salvation. (Phil. 1:6) We must "go on to perfection."

And why not? With the barrier of sin down, and the way opened to God (Heb. 10:20), there is no hindrance to a full life of fellowship with God. True, it must be, as Wesley pointed out, a moment-by-moment experience, and one may indeed "backslide," to use Wesley's own word, but one may be immediately reinstated by God and go on, as Paul went on, "toward the goal for the prize of the upward call of God in Christ Jesus." (Phil. 3:14) One will not claim perfection for himself—Jesus did not even acknowledge goodness (Mark 10:18)!—for such a claim invokes the pride which is the source of sin. Let others attribute perfection, if deserved, to the one who yearns for it, not as a selfish possession but as an unselfish passion, all his being desiring to "spend and be spent" for others (2 Cor. 12:15), "boasting" only of weaknesses that the "power of Christ may rest upon" him. (12:9)

There is a wonderful joy in complete commitment—and a wonderful assurance. "I bear on my body the marks of Jesus" (Gal. 6:17), said Paul. But he also said, "(Our) slight momentary affliction is preparing for us an eternal weight of glory beyond all comparison." (2 Cor. 4:17) And he added, "He who has prepared us for this very thing is God, who has given us the Spirit as a guarantee." (5:5)

We can see in all this what God is doing through his Spirit. And it gives us a clue to what God is like, at least in his relation to us. The doctrine of the Trinity has been taken to mean a description of God himself. But it is really an understanding of God as he has made himself known in the Bible. It is our discovery of him as Creator, and Savior, and Friend. It is a knowledge of God in the Biblical sense of the "I WILL BE" (Exodus 3:14), who makes known what he is by what he does for his children. And that is really all we know about God. As human beings we cannot know what God is "in himself." We can only know of "the God Who Acts." He acted in creation, making "the heaven and the earth" (Gen. 1:1)—and in salvation, present "in Christ reconciling the world to himself" (2 Cor. 5:19)—and now he acts in the Holy Spirit, guaranteeing "our inheritance until we acquire possession of it." (Ephesians 1:14) The doctrine of the Trinity is an outline of theology, a "theology of recital," because it tells of what God has done and is doing for us. Whatever more we may say of God, we cannot say less than this, the trinitarian manifestation of his love and concern.

8

THE KINGDOM AND THE CHURCH

Though the concept of a kingdom (the rule of a king) has yielded to other forms of government in recent times, there remains the necessity of some form of government in an organized society. In the story of the human race government began in tribalism where the chief was the authority. The ruler of a combination of tribes was called a king, and in time the rule attached to the kingly family and became hereditary. But uprisings sometimes displaced the ruling power with a military or a popular leader, and in our time such leaders have become dictators of one sort or another. But throughout all forms of government there has persisted the feeling that some kind of ruler, whether of personal or popular sort, whether hereditary or elective, was necessary to bring order out of the chaos which is the case when "everyone does what is right in his own eyes." (Jud. 21:25)

In primitive societies the tribal chief or king represented the god of the tribe and so was given divine honor. (I Sam. 10:1 & 24:6) Battles between tribes were really battles between the tribal gods who were regarded as the real rulers. (I Kings 20:23,28) Thus the real king of Moab was Chemosh Num. 21:29); of the Ammonites, Milcom (I Kings 11:5); of Syria, Rimon (II Kings 5:18); of Philistia, Dagon (Judges 16:25) . . . and where the god is not named in the Bible, the general term "baal" (lord) is substituted (Jud. 3:7), though, in Canaanite religion Baal was used as the personal name of a principal deity with many local designations. (II Kings 1:2; cf. Mark 3:22) In this context we understand the name given to the God of the Hebrews, YAHWEH, and the significance of the commandment, "You shall have no other gods before me." (Exo. 20:3) This means to honor Yahweh above all other gods. This worship of one God without denying the existence of other gods is called henotheism. It was the first form of Israel's loyalty to God. Later, this loyalty made him the Ruler of all people (Amos 9:7; chs. 1-2), and denied the existence of other gods. (Jer. 10:1-11) Yahweh was then asserted as the only God (Isa. 40:25-31), the one cause of all events (ch. 45). This is monotheism, the belief in only one God.

Yahweh was regarded from the beginning as the King of the Hebrews, Moses proclaimed Him as the God who had let the patriarchs, Abraham, Isaac, and Jacob, and would lead his people from Egypt. (Ex. 3:13-17) With Him Moses made a covenant at Sinai, formulated in "Ten Words" (Ex. 34:28n), and sanctified with a sacrifice. (Ex. 24:8) In His Name Joshua led the people into Canaan, the "Promised Land" (Josh. 4:21-24), and in His Name the tribal champions "judged" Israel. (Jud. 7:18) Samuel yielded to the demand for a king "like all the nations" (I Sam. 8:2), and when, at Yahweh's command he chose Saul—and later David—he "anointed" them (hence, the term Messiah which means "anointed": (I Sam. 10:1; 16:13) in the Name of "the Lord" who remained the King of His people, the earthly king being but His viceroy. (I Sam. 16:1) Israel was always a nation under God the King, and when, finally, it went down to defeat and into exile, it did not die for its God-King did not die. Jeremiah the prophet wrote the exiles saying, "I will be found by you, says the Lord, and I will restore your fortunes and . . . I will bring you back to the place from which I sent you into exile." (29:14) The Isaiah of the exile painted wonderful pictures of the restoration of Israel. (Isa., chs. 40-50) Like the sojourn in Egypt, the exile in Babylonia is a great turning point in the history of the Chosen People. From the one (c. 1200 B.C.) to the other (586 B.C.) there elapsed slightly more than 600 years, and from the exile to the time of Christ all but 600 years passed. The periods were, then, nearly equal in length.

But little is known of the post-exile period because it was a time of national eclipse. Though the Jews returned to the Promised Land, they were subjected first to the Persians (536-323), then the Greeks (323-168), then the Romans (63 B.C. on). A precarious independence was achieved by the revolt of the priest Mattathias in 168 B.C., which culminated in the "cleansing" of the Temple in 164, and was followed by the successive reigns of Mattathias' sons, Judas, Jonathan, Simon, the last initiating the Maccabean dynasty, all priest-kings. The exciting story is told in the apocryphal book of I Maccabees. It all ended with the Roman conquest under Pompey who, as the finally unsuccessful rival of Julius Caesar, coveted the glory of founding the Roman Empire. Such is the troubled time, full of oppression and disappointed hopes, that characterized the post-exile period of nearly 600 years.

But the Jews did not lose their faith. Three classes of leaders (Jer. 18:18) helped the people to hold on to it. The *priests* exalted the Mosaic Law and perfected the Temple ritual; the *wise men* were the philosophers who, beginning with common sense sayings or proverbs, finally wrestled with the problem of suffering (Job) and the meaning of life (Ecclesiastes), leaving a rich legacy of writings, including some Psalms (e.g., 37,73,139). The *prophets* first predicted the return from exile (Jeremiah, Ezekiel, II Isaiah), encouraged the rebuilding of the Temple (Haggai, Zech. chs. 1-8), and dealt with the problems of the returnees (III Isaiah, Zech. chs. 9-14, Malachi). But they increasingly turned to the visionary picturing of the supernatural Kingdom of God to be inaugurated by a defeat of the powers of evil and a revival of the People of Yahweh (Ezek. ch. 37) by resurrection (Daniel 12:2). This would be followed by a judgment (Dan. 7:9-10) in which the Kingdom would be "given" to the "saints of the Most High." (Dan. 7:22) The Kingdom would be an everlasting one (7:27) because it belonged to a "new heaven and a new earth" (Isa. 66:22; Rev. 21:1), a new creation to match the first creation which was corrupted with sin.

But who would be the viceroy-King in this Kingdom of God? The Son of Man, a supernatural figure who had the appearance of an ordinary man (hence, "son of man," (Dan. 7:13) and represented the "saints of the Most High."

It is easy to see how these ideas relate to the story of Jesus. Jesus himself rejected the idea of a Kingdom of David as an earthly kingdom like that of the ill-fated Macabees (Mark 12:35-37), and conceived his mission in terms of the Son of Man, a term used only by Jesus of himself, never (with the exception of Acts 7:56) by another of him. He did think of himself as the King-to-be when the Kingdom would be established. (Matt. 25:31; Mark 10: 37) In this sense he was the Christ, anointed by the Holy Spirit (Mark 1:10), God's Viceroy and therefore God's Son (Mark 1:11; ch. Psalm 2:7), certified as such by the Resurrection. (Rom. 1:4)

But here appears the greatness of Jesus' awareness of his mission and his consequent teaching. Greatness, he saw, inheres not in ruling but in serving (Luke 22:27; cf. John 13:1-5), even as a slave (Mark 10:44; Phil. 2:7), and before Jesus could be King of the Kingdom he had to be the Suffering Servant of God (Isa. 42; ch. 53), and give his life "as a ransom for many." (Mark 10:45; cf. Isa. 51:11) Thus Jesus transformed the idea of the King from that of a Ruler to that of a Servant-Savior (Mark 15:31-32), and the idea of the Kingdom from that of subject peoples to that of brothers and sisters in the Family of God. (Matt. 23:8-12) In his resurrection, as Paul points out, he became the "first-born among many brethren." (Rom. 8:29)

The Meaning of the Church

Thus we come to the meaning of the church in the New Testament. It is the fellowship of the redeemed, and its creation goes back to the Last Supper of Jesus with his disciples when he passed around the bread and wine in symbolic reference to his impending sacrifice for his own (Luke 22:28-30), saying "This is my Body . . . my Blood." His sacrificial act was certified as truly for God (Rom. 5:8) by his resurrection (Rom. 1:4), and its effectiveness for the disciples was assured by the gift of the Holy Spirit (Acts ch. 2: 15:8-9) as evidence of God's acceptance of them for Jesus' sake (Rom. 5:1-5)—and not only of them but of all who subsequently believe "in his Name." (John 1:12) To these disciples of Jesus the gift of the Holy Spirit is the "guarantee" (RSV) of their "inheritance" (Eph. 1:14) of eternal life (II Cor. 5:5; 1:22) which means life in the Kingdom in the age to come (John 3:4), though it begins as an experience here and now. (John 5:24)

The church, then, represents the Kingdom of God which is to come and yet is already here. It is to come because God will consummate the Kingdom in his own time (Mark 13:32; Acts 1:7) and in his own way. (Mark 10:40) In the New Testament the language of apocalypticism and its imagery is much used, but, as we have seen, Jesus, though he used it, was not bound by it, for, as in the case of other traditional material he transformed it in the light of his creative mission. He did believe, and teach, that it was God who would give the Kingdom (Luke 12:32), and not man who would "build" it. It was for believers to pray for it: "Thy Kingdom come" (Matt. 6:10), and to expect it (Luke 18:8), and to exemplify its life (this is the meaning of the "Sermon" on the Mount: (Matt., chs. 5-7). All this is the role of the church, the kingdom-society. The expectation of the Kingdom's consummation was, and must still be, of an imminent event. (Matt. 24: 36-44) As the kingdom-society the church lives on the alert, involved in this world but not committed to it as the final order, always eager for "the city whose builder and maker is God." (Heb. 11:10)

On the other hand, the church also represents the Kingdom which is already here. The Kingdom of God is now in our midst (Luke 17:21) in the living presence of Christ who now rules over us as the King of Love. (Gal. 2:20; 2 Cor. 5:14) By this Spirit we have power to overcome sin, the symbol of death (Rom. 8:2), so that the Life in the New Age (which is the Kingdom of God) is our life here and now (Rom. 8:12-14) as well as the promise of the life to come. (Rom. 8:10-11) The church, then, does not owe its life to this-worldliness but to God; nor is its existence justified by its mere social usefulness. It does indeed relate vitally to this world, and there is no human need which lies beyond the concern of the church. (Matt. 25:31-46) But its mission as the agency of the Kingdom is to transform the world through the power of God's Spirit. (Rom. ch. 12) It is in the world because, as long as the world exists, that is where it belongs. But it is not of this world. (John 17:15-16) It is of the world that is yet to be. (Heb. 11:13-16)

The Sacraments

In the light of the foregoing we understand the sacraments. To put the matter briefly, BAPTISM is the means by which we enter the Kingdom of God, and THE LORD'S SUPPER is the means by which we are nourished in the Kingdom-Life.

Baptism is by water and the Spirit (John 3:5), a rebirth

"from above" (3:3-7,31) into a new life by the power of God's Spirit. This new birth, it is made plain in John, is by understanding (3:10) that Jesus is the Son of Man (3:13), i.e., Son of God (3:16), whom to know is life eternal. Baptism, therefore, is a commitment to Christ as the revelation of God, and an opening of life thereby to the influence of God's Spirit. By that Spirit we are a "new creation" (2 Cor. 5:17) in anticipation of the New Creation which is the consummation of the Kingdom of God. (Rev. 21:1)

The *Lord's Supper* is the living observance of the Last Supper at which Jesus instituted the church as the Kingdom-Society through his sacrificial death. It is a memorial of his death, but more. It is a realization of his presence in his Living Body the Church. (1 Cor. 11:29) Oscar Cullman thinks that the prayer "Maran-atha" (Our Lord, come") was used at the original observance of the Lord's Supper to invoke the Living Presence of Christ. But the Lord's Supper is still more: it is a proclamation of "the Lord's death until he come" (1 Cor. 11:26), which means the consummation of the Kingdom. Thus this sacrament is a nourishment in the love of God made known to us in the death of Christ (Rom. 5:8) by which we are kept alive in the Kingdom of God until its glorious realization!

What of the additional sacraments offered in Catholicism and somewhat reflected in Protestantism: Confirmation, Marriage, Penance, Extreme Unction, Orders? These are a logical extension of the two sacraments which are the only ones mentioned as "ordinances" or directives of Jesus. (e.g., Matt. 2819; 1 cor. 11:25) *Confirmation* consummates the baptism administered to infants who as babies do not participate on their own but can, in confirmation, "renew the solemn promise that was made" by their parents or sponsors. *Marriage* is the solemnizing of the union God intends to be permanent (Mark 10:9), but nevertheless belongs to this life rather than life in the eternal Kingdom (Mark 12:25), and so is not properly a sacrament. *Penance* is the means worked out by the Catholic Church in history for the forgiveness of sin through the instrumentality of the priest as representing Christ. It is an ecclesiastical ordinance rather than the sacramental forgiveness by God's grace in baptism. *Extreme Unction* is mentioned as a ministry to the sick in James 5:14-15 with no mention of dying. The anointing of oil is accompanied by intercessory prayer for forgiveness. But this pastoral advice of James is neither an ordinance of Christ nor a sacrament of the Kingdom in which the believer already lives by God's grace whether in this world or the next. (2 Cor. 4:16-5:5) *Orders,* meaning ordination, developed as the means by which the clergy were distinguished from the laity as authorized to administer the sacraments. With the ordination by "laying on of hands" (Acts 8:18; 1 Tim. 4:14) was associated "apostolic succession," meaning the unbroken succession of such ordination from Christ through the apostles and their successors to the present. Ordination is not by man, nor the hands of men, but by the Spirit of God, that the church might be provided with the leadership needed (1 Tim. ch. 4; cf. 3:1-13) that "all things (might) be done decently and in order." (1 Cor. 14:40)

Has the church become too organized, too regularized, too structured to represent the dynamic expectation of the imminent Kingdom of God? It was inevitable that the church should have strengthened itself against evils within and attacks without. The collapse of the Roman Empire challenged the church even to save civilization, and it did so, bringing forth the impressive ecclesiasticism of the Middle Ages. But with this came the corruption of the church, and this called for a Reformation in the 16th century. Yet in the effort to reform itself the church also fragmentized, with the result that the Body of Christ was sadly torn apart. This was a new evil whose enormity is just now being realized.

To be true to its mission, the church must keep alive the

Spirit of Jesus, which is the Spirit of God (Rom. 8:9), and live not for itself but for the Kingdom. Its success is the Kingdom's success, and not that of its own human organization. Its preoccupation is with the realization of the Kingdom, and not of its worldly aggradizement. Its concern is with the saving of humanity to the life of the Kingdom, and not the mere saving of its own life. The saying of Jesus is as true of the church as of every believer: "Whoever would save his life will lose it; and whoever loses his life for my sake, and the gospel's, will save it." (Mark 8:35) That gospel is the Gospel of the Kingdom of God. (Mark 1:14-15)

9

THE CHRISTIAN LIFE

WHAT DOES IT MEAN TO BE A CHRISTIAN?

What does it mean to be a Christian? It certainly means knowing God as revealed in Christ, experiencing salvation from sin through the cross of Christ, and enjoying the privilege of God's presence through his Holy Spirit. These matters are discussed in the earlier chapters of this little book.

But does it mean an individualistic experience? Is one saved to and for his personal benefit? To become a Christian is indeed a personal matter, and the gospels tell a number of stories of Jesus' relating to individuals: Simon Peter (Luke 5:1-11), the sinful woman (Luke 7:36-50), Nicodemus (John 3:1-15), the Woman of Sychar (John 4:5-26), The man born blind (John ch.9), Martha and Mary (Luke 10:39-42), Zacchaeus (Luke 19:1-10), to mention no others. There are, in addition, the Resurrection appearances to individuals: Mary Magdalene (Mark 16:9), James, Jesus' brother (1 Cor.15:7); and, not least, Saul who, because God revealed his son to him (Gal.1:16), became Paul (1 Cor.15:8-9). In each of these cases Jesus connected with a personal need which related the believer to him as Savior. But he did not meet with universal response. We remember the case of the rich man who went away sorrowful because he found Jesus' invitation to follow him to be too costly (Mark 10:22). We think, sadly, of the disciples who were "with Jesus" (Mark 3:14) through his ministry and yet, in the one case, betrayed him (Luke 22:48) and, in the other, denied knowing him (Luke 22:61-62). Our response to Christ is dictated by our need, and our needs are variable and complex. But it must be said that it is the one who has a sense of need and discovers what Christ can do for him who becomes a Christian. Because of this, salvation is an intensely personal experience.

But does it end as an individualistic one? As we have seen, Jesus proclaimed the Kingdom of God, and died to establish it as a new covenant with God for his followers. God acknowledged Jesus' sacrifice as his own doing (Rom. 5:8) by honoring him with the Resurrection, and God acknowledged Jesus' followers as his covenant people by the gift of his spirit (Rom. 5:5). In this way the New Testament insists that salvation is not a matter of private interest merely, but a case of belonging to the Kingdom of God. One is saved for the Kingdom, and the benefit he derives from it is not primary but resultant. Since the church represents the Kingdom of God, one is saved to membership in the church, the church whose members God chooses by the gift of his spirit. This church is the Body of Christ (1 Cor. 1:27), and Christ is alive in it. To be in the Church is to be "in Christ," a phrase used as such or in equivalent form no less than 164 times by Paul in his writings! "For by one Spirit we (are) all baptized into one body," he says in (1 Cor. 12:13), and so we (collectively) are the temple of the Holy Spirit. (1 Cor. 3:16-17) Christ is related to this Body as the head to the physical body (Col. 1:18), or as a man to his wife, for "Christ loved the church and gave himself up for her" (Eph. 5:25), a tender figure of speech that derives ultimately from the prophet Hosea. (2:16-20)

The New Testament will not let us think of being Christian apart from the church. In spite of all the faults of the Corinthians, the Apostle Paul held up for them the highest image of the church and begged them to measure up to its meaning. Never once did he compromise his picture of the church as the Body of Christ.

The Christian life, therefore, is a life closely related to the church, to the people who are the church, and to the ministries of the church, in each of which we are personally involved.

Let us think of what these ministries are.

THE MINISTRY OF THE WORD

The Bible is the product of the church, not the church of the Bible. Even the Old Testament, which was the Christian Bible before there was a New Testament, resulted from the life of the chosen people as they were led by God through all the vicissitudes of their history. It was what God did, understood as his mighty acts by those who told of them, that eventually gave the people their Bible. This took place in three stages: the LAW in five books (Genesis to Deuteronomy)—the PROPHETS which included the prophetic histories (Joshua, Judges, Samuel, Kings) with the prophets: Isaiah, Jeremiah, Ezekiel, "the Twelve"—and the WRITINGS, including the Psalms, Proverbs and other Wisdom writings, the apocalyptic prophets, and the priestly histories, in short, the writings of the post exilic period. The authorization of Scripture is known as canonization, and such approved writings could be read in the synagogue services. The one criterion was that the Scriptures be inspired, which meant, for practical purposes, written in Hebrew by a well-known personage. The Old Testament was finally canonized by A.D. 90.

A similar process took place with respect to the New Testament. For nearly 20 years there were Christian churches without even a single epistle of Paul; there were 20 additional years before the first gospel was written; 30 more years before the last gospel was penned; another 50 years before the last New Testament book was composed. It was not until A.D. 367 that Athanasius of Alexandria listed for the first time the New Testament books exactly as we accept them. Again, inspiration was the basic requirement, and this meant connecting an acceptable writing with an apostle or his disciple. The New Testament was created by the church as an authoritative statement of faith to be read in Christian services.

This understanding of the origin of the Scriptures underlines the chief purpose of the Bible: to testify to the faith and to nourish believers in it by way of helping them in their Christian life in the church. The first thing Christians should do is read the Bible! Protestantism is founded on the authority of Scripture, not independently of the church but in support of it as the true expression of the Kingdom of God. Not the word of any man, but the Word of God is what the church needs! What cannot be justified by the Scripture cannot be justified, as Martin Luther insisted. But what is the Word, if it is not read? It is scandalous that Protestantism which began with the Bible, and championed the Scriptures in the language of the people, is now so widely represented by adherents who are largely ignorant of what is in the Bible.

But is the Word of God a matter of words in a book, merely? No. Paul reminds us that "the written code kills, but the Spirit gives life" (2 Cor. 3:6). The words convey the Word. The words are the vocabulary of God, but God speaks his own word. Therefore, the reading of the Bible is important as a possible encounter with God through his spirit, "for," as Paul explains, "the Spirit searches everything, even the depths of God" (1 Cor. 2:10—read vv.6 to 13). As Karl Barth emphasized, it is God's vertical transecting man's horizontal that constitutes the encounter which, as the verbal picture suggests, is, for the Christian at least, at the cross of Christ. Here at the climax of God's revelation is the crisis (a Greek word implying decision) which is involved in Christian experience. This experience begins with conversion but does not stop there. One "works out his salvation with fear and trembling, for God is at work in (our lives) to will and to work for his good pleasure" (Phil. 2:12-13). No doubt, there are encounters with God in all kinds of life-situations, but these are nearly if not wholly encompassed by the Bible in its manifold testimony to faith. Certainly the dimensions of the Christian experience are to be found in the "one Book" of which John Wesley spoke.

Neglect of the Bible is disastrous for the Christian and Christianity. Though an ancient book, written originally in language alien to us, needing repeated translation to keep abreast of our changing idiom, with strange names difficult at times to pronounce and ancient ideas that need updating to be comprehensible, all in all a Book that requires study with the help of commentaries or commentators, the Bible is nevertheless vital for the Christian life. Providentially, it is a Book of neither philosophy nor science, but a Book of life, the life of a People and of persons sensitive to God's leading, and it tells the story of the encounter with God in successive mighty Acts. It tells the story in vivid language, warm and human as well as inspiring and divine, and it can be read with immediate appreciation apart from all scholarly accomplishments. For we are there in the Bible. We find ourselves in its pages, and the Bible finds us in our condition. It points the way to salvation and growth in grace. We neglect it to our infinite and eternal loss.

THE MINISTRY OF WORSHIP

Christian Worship is the disciplined experience of God in fellowship with other believers in the life of the church, the Body of Christ. It grew out of earlier forms of worship in the experience of Judaism: the sacrificial worship of the

Temple and the devotional meetings of the synagogue. Hence, there are two basic elements in Christian worship: the liturgy of the Sacrifice of Christ (the Lord's Supper or Mass), and the liturgy of the Word of Preaching based on the Scriptures. (The word "liturgy" means "service," i.e., the serving of God.)

It was inevitable that the Last Supper of Jesus should become the Lord's Supper of the church. Connected, as it was in Christian thinking, with Jesus' Resurrection, the observance of the Lord's Supper naturally took place on Sunday ("the Lord's Day," Rev. 1:10), with the result that Christians substituted this day of Resurrection for the Jewish sabbath, especially after the destruction of Jerusalem in A.D. 70. They also came to understand that the sacrifice of Christ was the one Sacrifice for all time (Heb. 7:27) and replaced the on-going sacrificial system of Moses now made obsolete by God. (Heb. 9:11-14) The Lord's Supper then became an appropriation by faith (Heb. 10:22) of eternal sacrifice which opened the way to God for all believers. (10:19-20) Being not only Sacrifice but also High Priest, Christ ever "lives to make intercession" for us (Heb. 7:25; of. 9:24), which we may take to mean that Christ represents for us the eternal will of God to forgive by his grace, not our worthiness. (cf. Hosea 11:8-9) The meaning of Christ's Sacrifice is the historic demonstration of the steadfast love of God. The observance of the Lord's Supper is the appropriation of this love by faith.

One of the cardinal doctrines of the Reformation "the priesthood of all believers." By this Martin Luther meant not that each believer is his own priest before God, but that believers help each other in their Christian experience, in the spirit of Gal. 6:1. The minister, then, is not a priest but a leader, the servant of all (1 Cor. 9:19), specially trained and "set apart" by ordination in view of his gifts by God (cf. Gal. 1:15), and he leads the people in "corporate worship.

For the people are also called of God—"into the fellowship of his Son" (1 Cor. 1:9)—and are "called to be saints" (which means "set apart") for the service of God in the Body of Christ, the church. Here is another cardinal doctrine of Protestantism, the sacred calling of all believers, though, by the New Testament standard, this means primarily the call to be Christian, and not a blanket endorsement of the various "callings" of secular life. Christians are, indeed, to be conscientious about the work they do, and to do it "under God." that is, in relation to their calling as Christians, rejecting what is inconsistent with that calling.

From the beginning, then, Protestant worship was corporate. There is private prayer but not private worship in the strict sense of the word. "Worship," is indeed, "worthship," the giving of honor to God who is worthy of it, and this may be done privately in prayer. But private prayer, important as it is, is not to be substituted for the worship which is a function of the covenant community, the Body of Christ. In this the individual participates, but not for his own sake merely. He contributes in this way to the realization of the Kingdom of God on earth. The benefit he receives is derivative, not determinative. Thus attendance at worship does not depend on personal preferences the appeal of the minister, the inadequacy of this or that church member, the quality of the music, the character of the liturgy. These are important considerations but still only marginal. The best that man can do for God in worship is not too good, but the essence of worship is found in the simple gathering of "two or three" in the Name of Christ for the experience of his living Presence (Matt. 18:20), and the realization through him of God's steadfast love.

From the beginning, Protestant worship was Biblical. It was the Word of God, not of man, that was important. Preaching services came into existence, and "communion through preaching," as Henry Sloan Coffin captioned it in a book title, even tended to exclude the Lord's Supper, which in the freer churches was observed but once a month, or even quarterly. Such preaching services are in modern Catholicism represented by Bible Services with a homily. But their importance does not compare with the Mass for popular appeal. In Protestantism it is the other way around. The ultimate derivation of this kind of worship is the Jewish synagogue where there was the reading of the Law and the Prophets, an exhortation based on the lesson of the day (cf. Luke 4:16ff), the use of "benedictions" and prayers, and the giving of alms for the poor. The synagogue was a lay institution, ruled by elders with a president, and led by a rabbi or teacher. It grew up in the Dispersion of the Jews far from Palestine, who could not, of course, attend the Temple in Jerusalem except on rare occasions, perhaps only once in a lifetime. When Jerusalem fell and the Temple was destroyed in A.D. 70, it was the synagogue that saved Judaism from extinction. And it was the synagogue that was the model for Christian churches through the Roman empire.

Judging by a description of early Christian worship by Justin Martyr about the year 150, such a Bible service as the synagogue suggested was combined with an observance of the Lord's Supper together with the taking of an offering for orphans and widows, the sick and those in want, those in bonds and strangers—in short, "all that were in need." Thus the Communion "offering for the poor" goes back to earliest Christianity.

It may be said, in general, that Christian worship is ideally the combination of Bible preaching and the observance of the Lord's Supper. But no rigid distinction is to be made between the appropriation of God's love in the Supper as over against the exposition of the Word. Fundamental to both is the revelation of God in Christ and his cross, and the appropriation of this by faith. Here we understand the legitimacy of freer forms of worship. The Quakers have, from the beginning, practiced the "eloquence of silence." The frontier life of American history produced the camp meeting type or worship with its gospel-singing, its emotionalism, its altar call. In recent times, in both Catholicism and Protestantism, there has been experimentation in worship with new art forms, jazz music, informal observance of the Lord's Supper. Ascribing worth to God is, after all, a human endeavor and must be meaningful. The one essential is that it be a corporate endeavor, a participation in the Body of Christ as the reflection of the Kingdom of God where "the will of God is done on earth as it is in heaven."

THE MINISTRY OF PRAYER

Though private prayer is no substitute for worship, it is involved in worship, and, of course, essential for one's private life as a Christian. Corporate worship saves it from becoming a mysticism which tends to eclipse the individual person in a final "absorption" into the Deity. It also saves it from monasticism which is a withdrawal from others in a preoccupation with self. But, certainly, no group experience of worship can substitute for personal experience. Any corporate realization of God must be reflected in a personal appropriation and commitment. This is the meaning of the Psalms in the Bible. Corporate religion was the essence of Judaism, but the Psalmists found that, aware as they needed to be of how good God was to Israel, he was for that very reason good to them individually. In Psalm 22, referred to by Jesus in his cry on the cross (Mark 15:34), the agony of the sufferer is seen against the background of the "fathers" trust in God (v.4) and the psalmist vows to declare God's praise "in the great congregation." What sustenance this assurance offered Jesus in his suffering we can only guess, but it is a firm linking of the private and corporate experience of God.

This does not rob the individual of initiative before God,

nor the prophet of his responsibility to speak out God's will to a lagging people, nor Jesus to be what no other could ever be, the unique God (Luke 9:20). But it does prevent individualistic irresponsibility. Christianity begins with no one person's experience, nor ends with any one exemplar of it. Even Jesus carefully related his mission to what God had done before in the life of the Chosen People, and left his disciples with a fine sense of their corporate relation to the Kingdom of God (Luke 12:32). He also gave them a simple prayer which is couched in the plural, not the singular number.

This prayer might well be the pattern of private as well as public praying. It is "our (common) Father" we worship, whose Name we revere (above all our other loyalties), whose will we desire above our own (Matt. 26:39), whose providence we trust (Matt. 6:33), whose leading we follow, come what may, and whose glory we hope for in the final consummation when God will be "everything to every one" (1 Cor. 15:28). It is a Kingdom prayer. Its most difficult petition is the phrase, "Lead us not into temptation, but deliver us from evil." Shorn of its Kingdom-reference, this petition makes little sense. But "temptation" is the testing time when the weeds are separated from the wheat (Matt. 13:24-30), the sheep from the goats (25:31-46) at the Consummation— and "evil" is the Evil One whose power contests that of God in the struggle between good and evil in this world. The petition is a human one. We desire to be spared a testing we cannot survive and a power we cannot cope with in a life ultimately in the hands of God. The faith and hope of the early Christians was expressed in the words of (1 Cor. 10:13): "God is faithful, and he will not let you be tempted beyond your strength." Paul found in his own experience that in every trial God's grace was sufficient. (2 Cor. 12:7-10)

Thus, though one should never lose the corporate sense that is essential to Christianity, there is much need for private prayer, much joy and power in it. One cannot be a Christian without it. One cannot be saved in himself (Acts 10:30-31) or to the Kingdom of God (Col. 1:9-14) unless he makes use of private prayer.

THE MINISTRY OF SERVICE

Involved as it is with the Kingdom of God, the church is concerned with its proclamation in word and in deed, even as was Jesus. As his Living Body, the church continues Jesus' earthly ministry of preaching, teaching, and healing. In this ministry of service, the individual Christian as a member of the Body of Christ (1 Cor. 12:27) is necessarily included.

The Preaching Ministry

Preaching in the beginning meant proclamation: "Repent, for the Kingdom of God is at hand!" This implied evangelism, and it is to be noted that Jesus began where John the Baptist left off. (Matt. 3:2 & 4:17) Nor was the proclamation of the Kingdom left to Jesus and John; the disciples were sent out on such a preaching mission. (Matt. ch. 10) According to Luke, there was a second such mission enlisting no less than 70. (10:1-20) Evangelism, then, is the business of the laity as well as the clergy. Its essence is the challenging of every life to face up to God's immediate demand to acknowledge his rule, to repent of sin and be forgiven, to receive God's approval in the gift of his Spirit and acceptance for the Kingdom as represented by the church. The implications of evangelism are many, for the relating of life to God is fulfillment in every sense.

It is for this reason that the church invests all it does for humanity with the motive of evangelism. The church is not another social agency, even though there is no area of life in which it is not interested. Certainly it is concerned with the poor, the disinherited, the outcast—all this stems from the ministry of Jesus himself; but it is also concerned with the rich who are spiritually poor, the "ins" who are on the "outs" with God, the privileged who, like the haughty of old, really had nothing to boast of before God. (Matt. 3:9; James 5:1-6) The church does not see the disadvantaged as somehow made righteous by the lack of this world's goods, nor the advantaged as somehow proved righteous by their possessions. (Luke 12:15) It sees all men in need of the gospel of repentance and forgiveness, that the poor may have a new self-respect as redeemed by the grace of God, and the rich a new humility as needing no less to be saved by grace, a gift too expensive to buy. (Eph. 2:8-9) It is tragically true that life can be too hard (cf. Proverbs 30:7-9) and those so oppressed too dispirited to respond to any appeal to be saved by God's grace. Such grinding poverty, such crushing defeat it is surely the business of the church to attack, but the conditions improved, the work of the church is still not done. The persons so involved are still victims of sin that may actually be accentuated by the hard circumstances of their life, and they will need to be challenged to a better life under God, a life of new meaning and new responsibility and new satisfaction. Nevertheless, at the other end of the social scale the need may be as great in its own way. In an affluent society, it needs to be remembered that "the love of money is the root of all evil." (1 Tim. 6:10) Venality, bribery, profiteering, false advertizing, shoddy manufacturing, not to mention unrealistic salaries and wages, betting and all kinds of something-for nothing schemes, all testify to the power of money to substitute the material for the spiritual and to rob the soul of the values that are priceless. It is in precisely such a society that the gospel needs to be heard with clarity: "All have sinned and fall short of the glory of God, and must be justified by his grace as a gift through the redemption which is in Christ Jesus." (Rom. 3:23-24) Surely the main business of the church, and of every Christian, is evangelism!

The Teaching Ministry

The *teaching ministry* of Jesus has its counterpart in many of the church's services today. Much preaching today is properly classified as teaching. The Church School, whether on Sunday or during the week, in the church building or out of it, in formal or informal situations, is Christian teaching if it relates persons to God in an understanding of his will for life. It is commonplace to say that modern education, at all levels, owes its origin to early church schools and freely used the Bible as a first reader. Some of our older colleges began as seminaries for education of preachers. Other colleges began as church institutions.

But education today is going secular, and church-related institutions, including parochial schools, are having a hard time keeping up with the expensive education provided by the state. Yet the separation of church and state in America has excluded religious observances from the public schools even though in other areas of its life the state gives at least lip-service to God. Even in its missions at home and abroad, where the church provided the only schools there were in the beginning, the state has encroached to restrict what the church may do in educating the people.

Meanwhile our society is suffering from the lack of Christian education and the commitment that properly goes with it. Millions of young people never attend church or church school. Their religious knowledge, if any, is a pick-up of miscellaneous information and attitudes in a society still more or less infused with religious ideas and practices. It is a great problem. There is no substitute for Christian education. The situation is serious enough to challenge clergy and laity alike, and to call for new attempts at Christian education.

Certainly the Christian home needs to be made more aware of the need. Sunday Church School can be taken more seriously by teachers and pupils alike. Adult education, increasingly popular among all segments of the population, needs to be explored more fully for the opportunities it offers. The local church can do much more in special courses for its congregation, not only in Bible study but for the whole range of Christian life. An informed Christianity is its own best defense in a world where rival ideologies are challenging the Christian faith. Surely, every Christian has a responsibility in the church's teaching ministry.

The Healing Ministry

The *healing ministry* of Jesus is also represented by a variety of modern church services. Hospitals had their origin in the church during the Middle Ages. Concern for widows and orphans is specifically mentioned by James 1:27 as evidence of "religion that is pure and undefiled before God." Nursing as a profession still finds its inspiration in Florence Nightingale who, not yet 17, felt that God spoke to her, and at 30 noting in her diary that it was the age at which Christ began his mission, renounced marriage and dedicated herself to God's will. Medical science owes much to the Greek pioneers in medicine and surgery (as medical terminology abundantly testifies), but healing in the Christian sense is more than can be done for the body. The healing miracles of Jesus related the recipient to God by faith (Mark 5:34; 10:52), and his exorcisms were regarded by him as evidence of God's power at work in anticipation of the Kingdom (Luke 11:20), but in neither case was there guarantee of "results" (cf. Mark 1:34:6:5). The important thing was not the cure as such but the relating of life to God.

Christian healing, then, inheres in the relating of life to God—and its effect applies to mind as well as body. The troubled spirit is calmed and cured by faith, not without self-understanding. Here the psychologist or psychiatrist, as the case may be, has a role of play, but self-understanding alone does not heal. In the end the emotionally disturbed person must make a decision that enables him to be a responsible person again. The Christian decision is based on faith in God and his will for one's life. One gets himself off his hands into God's hands, and he is gloriously well!

But what of "faith-healing" as such? As a trick, as a means of getting only what one wants, as a short-cut it is to be suspected. It is not wise to dogmatize and say what may or may not be possible to faith. But surely it is Christian to say that God does not heal for our selfish ends but rather for his own righteous purposes. To claim a miracle is no small matter. The claim must relate not merely to what happened, but why. What is the claimant now doing for God with the renewed life given him? John Wesley, saved from the burning parsonage at the age of 6, felt he was "a brand plucked from the fire." But it was for the purpose God had in mind for his life. Surely that is more worthy of a miracle than the mere saving of one's skin for no particular reason. The whole life of Wesley was full of such miracles, lengthening his years to the ripe age of almost 88. Yet Jesus dies at 33. Who will say what God wills, or what God's specific purposes are?

Without denying the illimitable power of faith in God, the healing ministry of the church today is to cooperate with all the findings of science in offering to suffering humanity at home and abroad what it can do to make life better in the Name of Christ. In this ministry the motive is paramount: in the Name of Christ. It was so that Peter and John offered healing to the lame man at the Gate Beautiful of the Temple. (Acts 3:6) It is in the Name of Christ any one can offer a sufferer a cup of cold water (Matt. 10:42), or visit the sick and imprisoned (Matt. 25:36), or minister to orphans and widows. (James 1:27) For the wonderful thing is that Christ is himself in all the needy everywhere, and to help them is to help Christ. (Matt. 25:31-46) The healing ministry of the church is really the dignifying of life by identifying with its need and relating it to God by faith did Jesus. In this gracious ministry every Christian has a part.

THE MINISTRY OF MISSIONS

The threefold ministry of Jesus is fully represented in the church's ministry of missions. In primitive societies, especially, the church has been the means of introducing modern knowledge and technology. Church schools have been the only schools. Not infrequently the first reduction of a native language to written form has been by missionaries. Frank Lauback has been a pioneer in the spread of literacy by the method of "each-one-teach-one." Similarly the first modern dentist or doctor or nurse has in each case been a missionary, and the first hospital or dispensary a missions' one. While in many situations these ministries have been duplicated by local governments, the missions school or hospital continues as an important service, either as the best of the kind or the only such service for those not yet reached by government agencies.

As for the preaching ministry, it is on the mission field that preaching in the original sense of proclamation is mostly done. Evangelism is the heart of missions, and its result are native churches, organized pretty much as churches are on the home base. But the leadership is increasingly native, at all levels, so that missionaries serve under national superintendents or bishops to an increasing degree. In fact, it is the function of missionaries to work themselves out of the jobs they do by training local leadership to take over. The idea is to make Christianity indigenous in the hope that eventually western Christians the meaning of the faith in God through Christ for all the world!

For Christianity is not nationalistic or racial. It represents the Kingdom of God of which Jesus said, "They will come from east and west, and from north and south, and sit at table in the Kingdom of God." (Luke 13:29) Of the church Paul said: "There is neither Jew nor Greek, there is neither slave nor free, there is neither male nor female; for you are all one in Christ Jesus." (Gal. 3:28) This is the live issue in missions. Missionaries have been accused of being infiltrators for colonizing nations, and it must be admitted that earlier attitudes of superiority and the free resorting to armed protection from the home country gave some cause for the criticism. The policy of self-determination that followed World War I, and the dissolution of colonial empires, with the spawning of many small nations, that followed World War II, have seen the resurgence of non-Christian religions as an aspect of national pride, and the national imposing of many restrictions on missions. The general attitude seems to be: "We want what missions can do for us on our own terms by way of modernizing our countries, but we do not want to be propagandized on behalf of Christianity." Thus, though missionaries are not now seen as representatives of colonialism, they are still seen as essentially alien.

But the Great Commission still stands: "Go and make disciples of all nations . . . teaching them to observe all that I have commanded you." (Matt. 28:19-20) Is there any compromise with this word of the Risen Christ? No. As we have seen (Ch. IV), Christianity does not consider all religions as equally true or equally effective, and feels obligated to bear its own witness in accord with Christ's command. This means not merely its social services, but its proclamation. It will teach and heal, but in the Name of Christ—and it must preach that there is no other Name given among men whereby we must be saved. (Acts 4:12) This is a matter of honest conviction. It can be said without haughtiness and in humility, with appreciation of the worth of other cultures, other religions. It can be said with a willingness to learn, even to the point of being proved wrong should that be the case in the end!

Meanwhile, there seems to be no other course then to explore every legitimate opportunity to evangelize the world, to provide in the Name of Christ the services humanity needs for its help, to extend Christ's Kingdom of Love to all peoples and all races, to show to the whole world that, grevious as may have been the faults of imperialism and the shortcomings of the church, the church does intend nothing but the good of all human beings as equally the children of God. In a significant way, the international, interracial, intersocial church is the dawning of the new day of peace. The angel-song at Jesus' birth, "Peace on earth, (God's) good will among men" (Luke 2:14 mg), may yet be heard around the world with new hope; Christ, "the Prince of Peace" (Isa. 9:6), may yet rise as "the sun of righteousness . . . with healing in its wings." (Mal. 4:2) Certainly, the church represents something other and better than the United Nations, indispensable as that organization is. A forum of conflicting world opinion is one thing, but a "brotherhood uniting all mandkind in service and in love" (as the pledge of the Christian Flag puts it) is something better. A balance of terror, in view of the nuclear bomb, may provide a peace of fear; but mutual respect, based on the common Fatherhood of God, can give the peace of heaven on earth, for "the Kingdom of God is . . . righteousness and peace and joy in the Holy Spirit." (Rom. 14:17) What apology has Christianity to make for showing the nations the way out of the animosities and conflicts that have, as the Preamble to the United Nations charter puts it, "brought untold sorrow to mankind"? And what Christian can stand aloof from a ministry that involves the very existence of mankind?

THE STEWARDSHIP LIFE

The Christian is not a free man. His life is not his own, for it was bought with a price (1 Cor. 6:19-29). He belongs to Christ. He is a member of Christ's Body, the church. He is involved in the work of the church because the church is the Body of Christ at work in the world today. Any one who considers himself saved for his own benefit is not saved at all. If he is saved, he is saved for service. The strange, but true arithmetic of Christianity is that he who loves his life finds it (Mark 8:35), he who gives gets more than he gives Luke (6:38), he who dies rises to a greater usefulness here and hereafter. (John 12:24-25) Yet all this is not calculation; it is not a bargain struck with God. It is a commitment that yields results that can not be predicted but are as inevitable as God's generosity. (Mark 10:28-31)

These considerations suggest the life of stewardship. This is frequently spoken of in terms of God's ultimate ownership of all we possess. We owe God a return on his investment, as it were. (Matt. 25:14-30) The 10% "interest" suggested as our obligation derives from Malachi 3:8 which speaks of robbing God of the "tithes and offerings" which are his due.

Without denying the cogency of this understanding, which has the merit of plain, practical speaking, let it be said that the Christian commitment is a greater and a deeper one. We hold back nothing from God. We invite God to claim us fully: our thoughts and desires as well as our talents and possessions. We not only give him what we can of our substance for his work in the world, but we ask him to control what we keep, and to help us use it conscientiously. We recognize his special interest in the one day in seven set aside for his worship, but we ask him to help us keep the whole day holy and to sanctify every day with his presence. We not only do "religious work," in or for the church, but we try to relate our faith to all our work, and, if we are convinced that what we make a living at is really not in keeping with our living as Christians, we give it up, perhaps at great financial sacrifice. We use church envelopes and put an offering in the plate and perhaps keep an account of our other benevolences for income tax purposes, but we do not thereby credit ourselves with a corresponding degree of righteousness. We want our commitment to be joyous because it is not calculated.

It is really a question of character. What kind of person is the Christian? What habits characterize him? What allows him to do what others do, or keeps him from going along with the crowd?

Certainly, there must be individual differences. Each person must be himself, and there is no yardstick by which all are equally measured. For God did not pour us all into the same mold. Character is basically the translation of one's thoughts into words and deeds, the involvement of one's life in the life of others in helpful ways, especially in the ministries of the church.

The point is that we take God seriously. We are most serious about that which affects our bank balance. (Matt. 6:21) But our spending patterns only reveal what really lies in our heart. We say with Paul, "The life I now live by faith in the Son of God who loved me and gave himself for me. It is no longer I who love, but Christ who lives in me." (Gal. 2:20)

That is the wonderful life of stewardship.

10

THE PROBLEM OF SUFFERING

The greatest problem for the Christian faith, and the most difficult aspect of Christian living, is the grim fact of suffering. Why in a world made by a supposedly good God should there be suffering? Why should dedicated people, devoted to the service of God, have, as did Paul, a "thorn in the flesh"? Why should babies die before they have a chance to live, or adults live who would rather be dead because of a debilitating handicap? Why should the human mind go beserk with behavior as violent as it is senseless, or why should the human body destroy itself, its our mechanisms gone out of control? Why should man be inhuman to man in a world racked by devastating war, and in a society scarred by public and private cruelty? The list seems endless, and the agony beyond calculation. It is vividly captioned by the loud cry of Jesus on the cross (the only "saying" recorded in Matthew and Mark): "My God, my God, why . . . ?"

Desperate answers have been given for the bitter "Why?" Some have said there is no God—but that leaves the cosmological question unanswered: "Why is there a world at all?" Others have said that God is not good or at least he is indifferent and unconcerned about human suffering. But that leaves ignored the existence of the actual good, in the world and in human nature. Does it not belong? Is it a strange defiance in a hostile world? Which is more fundamental: the good or the bad? Can we better explain the bad as the absence of the good, or the good as the absence of the bad? Others have suggested that God represents the good in the midst of the bad, and that the suffering we know is the reflection of a cosmological struggle in which God himself is engaged. This dualism, as it is called, is found in the New Testament. God is there said to be opposed by Satan (the Devil) who with his minions, the demons, is currently in control of the world. (Eph. 6:12) The exorcism of demons by Jesus and the apostles was regarded as the beginning of the final struggle in which Satan would be overthrown (Rev. 12:7-9), cast out of heaven to be defeated on earth in the final Armageddon (Rev. 16:12-16), after which God's good rule would be established for ever in the New Age.

Thus the New Testament in its own way is fully aware of the problem of suffering, seeing it as indeed a problem for God, but not greater than God's power to overcome. Perhaps there is no human explanation for the existence of evil. Studdert-Kennedy, who as a British Army chaplain struggled with the problem of suffering in the midst of war, wrote poignantly: "The ultimate problem, the problem of evil, is insoluble . . . But our job is not to solve the problem of evil but to destroy evil and blow the problem up!" But we cannot destroy evil. We may ameliorate it, and must do what we can as "children of the light" and not of darkness but in the end the problem is God's, and he alone can abolish evil. Meanwhile, we must live with what we cannot change, and find, with Paul, that God's grace is sufficient for us because his power is made perfect in our weakness. (2 Cor. 12:9)

Can we discern the limitations belonging to this life which sometimes cause suffering? It would seem, for one thing, that we are absolutely dependent on our bodies, and our bodies are, in turn, subject to mechanical factors that have nothing to do with our character as children of God. There is no other way for us to live in this world. We are conditioned by heredity (which may give us a physical weakness: hemophilia is a case in point). We may lose a limb in an accident and be unable thereafter to do some things we once did. We may have a "cerebral accident" (meaning a stroke) because of weakened arteries and may die from it, or, worse in some cases, not die from it. To be sure, some of these conditions may be traced to a "bad" heredity by which "the sins of the fathers are visited upon the children, if not by "acquired characteristics" then by social factors of a hereditary sort. Or evil may result from our own bad performances, our sinfulness, carelessness, insensitivity, and we ourselves are responsible for it. But the basic fact remains: we need our bodies to live in this world, and, as in the case of the virtuoso who selects a perfect violin in order to play his best, we must have bodies equal to the demands of our best intentions for us to live well.

Again, we live in a world along with other people. "It is not good that the man should be alone," God says in Gen. 2:18, and he provided man a "helpmeet" (KJV). "God gives the desolate home to dwell in," we read in Psalm 68:6, which in the King James Version is translated, "God setteth the solitary in families." He has placed families in society, and society in national settings, nations together in a world. We want it that way. The advantages of togetherness far outweigh the advantages of loneliness. But we are bound to each other in a mutuality that can be a disadvantage at times, even harm and death. Thus on the highway we can be killed or crippled by an irresponsible driver. On the street or in our social contacts we can "pick up a germ" we do not want. We can be the victims of the criminally-minded. Our spirits can be crushed by those who despise us or just ignore us. Our families can be broken by divorce, or divided by quarrels. Our society can be riven by strife, and our world ruined by war. Yet we cannot retreat from the world. Even if we can, as did Thoreau, retreat to the woods for a time to escape the life of "quiet desperation," we do not want it as a steady diet. Most of us do not see the comparative advantage of lonely living. We are made for each other, to live together as brothers should, and to suffer together if we must.

Once again, we live on the human level where suffering is more intense than at the lower levels of life. Here we speculate, of course, but it would seem that animals do not have the range of suffering characteristic of human beings. No doubt, animals suffer too much, and that mostly from human animals, and so there is need for the Society for the Prevention of Cruelty to Animals. But, with their limited power of thought and their larger dependance on instinctive behavior, they do not worry ahead of time about what may happen, nor afterwards about what has happened. They do not complicate their lives with vain regrets, or add to their mental burdens sympathetic identification or vicarious suffering. They are not concerned with sin and a guilty conscience, with death and sorrow, with God and the meaning of life. Fear they have, but not as complex as ours; instinct they have, but not our power of choice nor our "sense of ought." Yet we cannot be different from what we are. We really do not want to be. We would rather endure the kind of misery that is our lot as humans than relax in the kind of thoughtlessness that is the lot of animals. Do we want to be free of pain and worry to the extent that we desire to give up the Christ who cared so much he sacrificed himself on the cross for our sakes? He did it as a human for us humans, and he challenges us to join him in rising to the height of our humanity with God's help (Mark 10:27), and to share his cross with him.

Here we come to the positive function of suffering. Did God put us here, as one has expressed it, to enjoy ourselves or to have ourselves? Perhaps the kind of world we live in is designed to develop character. Where the conditions of existence are real and not a pretense; where consequences are "for keeps" and not "for fun"; where God does not rush in at any time to bail us out of trouble—in just such a world we must take life seriously and accept responsibility earnestly. If there are those who are victims of circumstances beyond their control, all that we are as human beings urges us to help because we ourselves would want to be helped. We cannot ignore the needy without a feeling of guilt—if we are normal. If there are those who carelessly and lawlessly hurt others, then we as humans must devise laws and controls to minimize the harm so caused. If the very nature of human life makes suffering most intense, then as humans we must develop new understandings and new kinds of helpfulness. If we do not make good at the human enterprise, what may we hope of God for what may lie beyond? In suffering and death we learn the real meaning of life.

All this does not mean that God does not care and does not concern himself with our situation. God does make himself known in Christ, and Christ does identify with "the last, least, and lost" of the human family. God is concerned with human sin, its pride and selfishness, and knows how deeply it is implicated in the experience of suffering. The material (mechanical) conditions of our earthly existence stand unchanged, but the sinful conditions should not. It is these that God attacks in a strange and wonderful way: allowing his Christ to suffer by them, be put to death by evil-doers, a real death that meant under the conditions the dreadful feeling of God-forsakenness: "My God, my God, why hast Thou forsaken me?" This is the meaning of sin! This is what we must know! This is what God makes known in the cross of Jesus. But he makes known in the same cross the love that accepted it: "Jesus . . . having loved his own . . . loved them to the end." (John 13:1) So the God, who is revealed in Jesus, loves his human children even to the end, and joins them in suffering! This is the ineffable truth of the Christian revelation, so unbelievable to non-Christians, yet so real to suffering humanity. The cross has always been the inspiration of sufferers, and the God who has seemed too far away to be concerned becomes the God-in-Christ to those who must see him through their pain and their tears.

Suffering is indeed a problem to Christian faith, but one that is gloriously illuminated by the cross. This is why in John 12:23 Jesus says, "The hour has come for the Son of Man to be glorified"—glorified, not defeated. Suffering is a problem to the Christian life, but one that is bearable in the thought that God himself is involved in it. This is why in John 13:31, Jesus says, "Now is the Son of Man glorified, and God is glorified in him." God is glorified strangely, wonderfully, in our suffering, whatever it is, for God has the power to change it, transform it, make it serve a useful purpose. So Paul says, "In everything God works for good with those who love him." (Roman 8:28)

11

THE GOAL OF OUR STRIVING

The Gallup opinion poll shows more people to believe in God than believe in life after death. That is understandable, even commendable. To believe in God as the ultimate reason for this world and to find him necessary to one than to believe that he is so important that he must live for ever. There are those who say they do not want immortality; when they die they want to stay dead!

In the long run, it is not what we want but what God wants for us that determines the matter. We did not ask to live this life; we came alive and found ourselves here! It does not matter whether we would rather be dead; we are not. There are some who cannot take it and finally commit suicide, hoping to "end it all." But these persons are considered abnormal. They are considered "sick." The law even considers them guilty! We are supposed to accept life as "right" and death as "wrong." Life is the gift of God and no man may take even his own life without doing wrong.

Nature is full of marvelous illustrations of the triumph of life over death. Even after twenty-three atomic and hydrogen bomb blasts over a period of twelve years, Bikini Atoll recovered so much in the next ten that in 1968 the inhabitants were allowed to return to a home land relatively free of radiation, thickly covered with undergrowth, and capable of growing cocoanut palms and other plantings. Surtsey Island, off the coast of Iceland, born of volcanic eruptions from under water over a 4-year period (1963-67) began, even before it had wholly cooled, to receive, by ocean and air and bird droppings, mosses and lichens and hardy plants that got a determined foothold on its inhospitable lava and volcanic sand. Life is the standing miracle of this earth. And now it is the prime question in the minds of the space explorers.

Despite the few who try to make a virtue of death, life is the persistent concern of humanity: "All that a man has he will give for his life." (Job 1:4) Self-preservation is a fundamental instinct. "If a man die, shall he live again?" (Job 14:14) is a question that never ceases to be asked. The overwhelming testimony is that man does want to go on living. All over the world, among the most primitive peoples, and as far back as the evidence may be found, back beyond history amid the diggings of archaeology, there is manifested the desire for life after death. Hindus believe that one returns to this world in another form of life, perhaps that of an animal, in accord with his just deserts. The ancient Greeks thought of the immortal soul that occupied perishable bodies in successive generations. Many ancient peoples had some notion of Hades (Hebrew: Sheol), the abode of the departed who were neither dead nor alive but mere shades of their former selves. (Isa. 1:9-20) Unable to conceive of a satisfactory after-life, they were at least unwilling to surrender the thought of life altogether.

Not only in nature, then, but also in human nature the insistence on life runs strong. Why? At the human level life means more than simple functioning (going through the motions of living). Life means a precious personality, the unique individual who is really irreplaceable. There is no substitute for one's father or mother, one's husband or wife, one's son or daughter, one's brother or sister—or even of oneself. In nature, as Tennyson observed, the species may be more important than the individual, but it is not so when human love is eternal. Love without persons to love or be loved is non-existent. There is a deep revulsion in human nature to surrendering an infinitely precious person to the ground as if the inert earth were the last word in existence.

There is also the question of character which deserves more recognition than this short life can give it. Here the moral sense is outraged. How can the good and bad, the helpful and predatory, the conscientious and conscienceless, find but a common end? It does not make sense. If the final verdict in life is the inescapable grave, it is a mockery of all our justice and points to but one desirable: to get all one can by any means possible regardless of all moral considerations. This is as a matter of fact, the philosophy of some: "Let us eat and drink, for tomorrow we die." (I Cor. 15:32) The problem is not simply that of equality of reward. It is the far more basic question whether life is serious about virtue. By no honest reckoning is virtue its own reward in this life. It must be rewarding beyond this life. It is noteworthy that Jesus invoked reward as a real consideration in connection with the good life. He recommended the kind of living that was noted secretly by the Father in heaven who would not fail to reward. Is this a calculating ethic? No. It simply insists that there is a final justice because God is just, even if in this world there is injustice because man is unjust.

There are those who minimize this consideration by appealing for vindication to humanity as a whole and to history. This is a high-minded humanism and deserves serious consideration. But it is an ultimately vain hope, for the world and all its works will cease finally to exist. This may be said to make no real difference since all that we do is justified by the benefit it is to mankind, and if the human race no longer needs it, it will have served its purpose. Shall we say, then that justice is somehow satisfied even though the net result of the effort is zero? That hardly commends itself to the absolute demand of justice itself.

The problem is really that of individual worth. There is

no virtue apart from the persons who practice it. When the the persons go, virtue like love disappears. All the values that make life worth while depend on the persons who exhibit them. More than that, each person is a unique combination of values, for this is the only way values can exist. All the good therefore that God desires depends on the good people who do it. Is God not serious about this? The Christian hope says he is. It insists that the individual person is so important to God that his final destiny is not, as the mystical faiths assert, absorption into the deity, there to be lost as a drop of water in the ocean. On the contrary, the unique person whom God loves, and for whom Christ died, lives forever, his own authentic self, sustained by God, always distinguishable from God, in a person-to-person relationship with God after death as before.

The whole question is one of God's character and purpose. If God made us in his image to have fellowship with him, then he did not make us as play-things to discard but as persons of infinite worth to live with him in the "Father's house" (John 14:2) for ever. Can we say less of God than this and still call him God the Father? Can we take seriously a God who would bring a world, and life into existence and, after all this, make nothing permanent of it? Not so did Paul read God's purpose. He saw in the limitless future surprising possibilities as the consummation of God's intention. (1 Cor. 2:9)

This limitlessness of God's purpose is reflected in our own feeling about life. Do we not say of so many who die: "He had so much to live for." Do we never feel of even ourselves that Victor Hugo said of himself: "I have not said the thousandth part of what is in me. When I go down to the grave I can say, like many others, 'I have finished my day's work.' But I cannot say, 'I have finished my life.'"

It seems clear that nothing short of eternal life is consistent with the character and purpose of our God. But how is it possible? This is perhaps our chief difficulty. We know life only in connection with a physical body, and we know the body dies. How then can there be life after death?

As we have seen, the ancient Greeks taught that the soul (being a bit of the divine) would not die, and so lived on to occupy successive mortal bodies. This is not the teaching of the apostle Paul who held that life after death is by resurrection, God giving us a body like Christ's glorious body. (Phil. 3:21) The resurrection-power of God's Spirit (Roman 1:4) is already at work in us, and it is this power that carries us beyond physical death to life in the New Age. That is the meaning of "eternal" life. The word does not mean "everlasting," which is a different Greek word. "Eternal" is the adjective form of the Greek word meaning "age." Eternal life is, then, the new-age life, when God will have created a new heaven and a new earth. (Rev. 21:1) That the resurrection of the resurrection of Christ himself, may not await the New Creation is suggested by the saying of Jesus from the cross: "Today, you will be with me in paradise (Luke 23:43), and Paul's own expressed hope: "To depart and be with Christ . . . is far better? (Phil. 1:23)—although Paul also mentions the 'general resurrection.'" (1 Thess. 4:16)

But is all this a realistic conception of the "how" of life after death? Certainly, we need bodies on earth in order to express our personalities. And certainly there are spiritual dimensions to our earthly existence. We can hardly say that the brain is the mind with its non-physical ideas, its hopes, fears, duties, appreciations, memories, plans, and so on. We cannot say how much of our bodies we need in order to be whole persons. Helen Keller, though blind and deaf, achieved an amazingly full life. The one who loses a limb or two in an accident or in battle is not reduced as a person by the degree of bodily injury. Yet we need our bodies in order to be persons. The interrelation of body and soul in this life supports the Pauline concept that in the life to come we shall not be disembodied spirits. But beyond this we cannot go.

We must accept what we cannot explain. The fact that is eternal life does not depend on us but on God. If we believe God intends it, we can believe that God can implement it. Our hope is not in man but in God.

There is a final consideration: what of heaven and hell? The art and literature of the Middle Ages offered the people sumptuous glimpses of heaven and painted lurid scenes of hell, but the New Testament actually gives us but little information. What it does give is not definitive description but symbolic suggestion. For want of specifies it seems best to think of life after death as a continuation of life before death but on a spiritual plane. If we grow in grace there as here, we begin there where we leave off here. In a real sense, we make our own heaven and hell by what we take into eternal life. Symbolized as the Fathers' House (John 14:2) in which the glory of God is the only light (Rev. 21:23), those who want nothing to do with God would in his blazing presence be in hell. In any case, the notion of physical space is hardly in order for a spiritual existence. One symbol for hell is that used by Jesus: "Behenna." (Matt. 5:29-30) This meant the Valley of Hinnom (Ge Himmon) south of Jerusalem where the citys' waste was dumped. This symbol suggests that hell is for those who have made themselves useless to God—and it is a grim picture, as it should be. What Paul says is: "The wages of sin is death—but the free gift of God is eternal life in Christ Jesus? (Roman 6:23)

Our eternal destiny depends on what we do on earth. And the quality of what we do is measured by our relationship to Christ. Having done our best in fellowship with him, we leave to God what he will do for us beyond our earthly pilgrimage. (Hebrew 11:13) But we are not worried. For God is the Father of our Lord Jesus Christ—and our Father too.

12

THE ECUMENICAL CHURCH

The scandal of Christianity is that it is so divided. In our consideration of the church's ministry of missions, we spoke of international Christianity as the pattern of world-wide peace, but the unlovely truth is that in some respects Christianity is as shot through with rivalries and conflicts as is the United Nations. How can the church recommend to others what is does not itself practice? How can it even be sure of its existence in view of the saying of Jesus himself: "If a kingdom is divided against itself, that kingdom cannot stand." Mark 3:24) How can God, through the church, grant the petition of Jesus respecting not only the original disciples but also "those who are to believe in me through their word . . . that they may all be one . . . so that the world may believe that Thou has sent me"? (John 17:20-21)

The situation is not as bad as it was. Many mergers of denominations have taken place including that which makes ours The United Methodist Church. In Division One of our Constitution, Article V deals with Ecumenical Relations and says: "As part of the Church Universal, The United Methodist Church believes that the Lord of the church is calling Christians everywhere to strive toward unity and therefore it will seek, and work for, unity at all levels of church life: through world relationships (within its own fellowship), through councils of churches, and through plans of union with churches of Methodist or other denominational traditions." As part of our Constitution, ecumenism becomes a permanent concern of United Methodism.

Of course, the impulse to unity has been growing for years. It first expressed itself in efforts outside of the organized churches. The British and Foreign Bible Society was created in 1804, and was followed by the American Bible Society in 1816. The Young Men's Christian Association, undenominational, was founded by George Williams in London in 1844, the Young Women's Christian Association in 1855. The Young People's Society of Christian Endeavor was formed by Francis E. Clark in 1881, and the Student Volunteer Missionary Movement was launched in 1886. There has been much cooperation in Sunday School work from the days of the American Sunday School Union early in the 19th century. The Women's Christian Temperance Union and the Anti-Saloon League are also historic examples of interdenominational cooperation.

A real break for church united was made with the formation in 1908 of the Federal Council of Churches of Christ in America, whose purpose was to find practical ways for denominations to work together. The Federal Council became the National Council in 1950, and all churches belonging to it subscribe to the basic faith in Jesus Christ as "Divine Lord and Savior." But it is important to note that, though originally Protestant, the Council now includes Eastern Orthodox churches of different language traditions: Russian, Ukrainian, Rumanian, Syrian.

The first attempts in the direction of a unified, world Christianity were made, significantly, on the mission field where denominational rivalry and conflicting representations of Christianity were confusing to the non-Christian mind. A number of denominational boards agreed not to duplicate efforts anywhere. Existing work was not abolished but new work avoided the invasion of territory already being evangelized by an established mission. There were exceptions, of course, but the idea, once enunciated, recommends itself. Interdenominational missionary gatherings were held beginning as early as 1854 when Alexander Duff made a visit to America. This conference was followed by others in Liverpool (1860), London (1878, 1888), New York (1900), the last attended by nearly two thousand Christian workers from all over the world. A most significant conference was held in Edinburg in 1910 which eventuated in the International Missionary Council which held important meetings in Jerusalem (1928) and Madras (1938-39). The Edinburg assembly was the inspiration also of two significant movements, one on the Life and Work of the Churches which held a conference at Stockholm in 1925, and the other on Faith and Order (doctrine and organization) of the Churches which held its first meeting at Lausanne in 1927. It was these conferences which led to the organization of the World Council of Churches in Amsterdam in 1948. There three hundred and fifty-one delegates from one hundred and fifty-two churches in forty-four countries voted it into existence on August 23. Dr. John R. Mott, a great Methodist layman, long active in ecumenical movements, was named honorary president. John Foster Dulles, the Presbyterian layman who later became Secretary of State for the United States, made a significant address in which he said: "This Assembly of the Churches has world-wide significance. . . . We are here to create a world organization that will go on working daily to mobilize Christian power to break down the walls of division. Thus we shall serve him who was lifted up that he might draw all men unto him."

At its third Assembly at New Delhi in 1961, the World Council welcomed into its membership the Russian Orthodox Church, and included one hundred and ninety-seven member churches in ninety countries and territories representing over three hundred million Christians. It adopted as its credo the definition of the General Secretary, Visser 't Hooft: "The World Council of Churches is a fellowship of churches which confess the Lord Jesus Christ as God and Savior according to the Holy Scriptures and therefore seek to fulfill together their common calling to the glory of one God, Father, Son and Holy Spirit." At the same time, the International Missionary Council integrated with the World Council.

The next great ecumenical step came in 1962 when Pope John XXIII called together the ecumenical council of Roman Catholic prelates known as Vatican II. The purpose was symbolized by the Italian word *aggiornamento* which means a modernization or updating with the thought of renewal. A new attitude of openness now characterizes Roman Catholicism, which is now seeking fruitful contacts with Protestants and non-Christians. It is not that Catholicism is "going Protestant" or has devised a clever scheme to trap Protestants into its grasp—these are wholly unworthy reactions to what must be regarded as the work of God. Pope John, whose instincts were pastoral, and Catholic scholars were fully aware of what was happening both inside and outside of the immediate orbit of Roman Catholism, and felt the time had come for a reassessment. Who will say what the end-result will be? The Vatican Council welcomed Protestant observers, including outstanding Methodists, and the Roman Catholic Church has sent observers to meetings of the World Council of Churches. Pope Paul VI, who succeeded Pope John on June 21, 1963, has assumed a world-concern like no Pope before him, and has championed peace for all peoples, regardless of faith. It is most significant that the largest single body of Christians is moving toward a realization of Christ's hope of a unified church for a fragmented world.

A significant Protestant effort was initiated by Eugene Carson Blake, Stated Clerk (at the time) of the United Presbyterian Church, when he preached a sermon in Grace

Cathedral of the Protestant Episcopal Church, San Francisco, in December, 1960. He made the bold proposal that the United Presbyterian Church, the Protestant Episcopal Church, the United Church of Christ, and the Methodist Church, meet to form a plan of church union both Catholic and reformed, and at the same time invited other denominations to join in the effort. The Disciples of Christ and the Evangelical United Brethren Church (this was before the forming of the United Methodist Church) did become part of The Consultation on Church Union (COCU), as it was called. It came officially into being in Washington in 1962, and the consultation has since met annually receiving reports from study commissions. There are difficult problems to solve concerning the relation of Scripture and tradition, the ministry and ordination, worship and the sacraments, the government of the church. Differences of opinion root in loyalty to historic traditions, and cannot easily be resolved. Each denomination likes to feel that it represents real Christianity, that its sacraments are what Christ intended, that its government is what New Testament approves, that its worship is the true vehicle of God's Spirit. It is difficult to concede that a denomination other than one's own may have in its tradition elements of truth needing recognition. It is not so simple a matter as finding the greatest common denominator, because conflicting views can be mutually exclusive. Wesley's break with "apostolic succession" is a case in point. That God has blessed the ministry of those who, lay as well as clerical, do not stand in the historic chain of "laying on of hands" is not to be denied—the question is how it should be done in a united church, and what recognition can be given those now functioning who cannot believe that they have been but pretenders to the gifts of God's Spirit. Similarly, how can modes of baptism be reconciled, if at all. And how can the Lord's Table be open to all believers when all do not have the same understanding of Communion? The watchwords of COCU need to be taken seriously by all concerned if progress is to be made. The first is "truly *catholic*," meaning a church united in loyalty to one Lord Jesus Christ (the word "church" derives ultimately from the Greek word, *kyrios*, meaning "lord"—and the word "catholic" means "universal" suggesting that there is really only one church. The second word is "truly *reformed*," meaning a church that cherishes the insights gained by the Reformation: that God spoke and speaks in the Scriptures and the church must be ready today to listen afresh to the Word of God. The third word is "truly *evangelical*," meaning a church that is more concerned to save the world in the name of Christ than to save itself. This is not the place to suggest solutions, based on these watchwords, to the problems COCU faces. These solutions will be provided, if possible, by those charged with the responsibility by their respective denominations.

The sum of the matter seems to be that we are dealing with what man has done with the church which God has given to the world through Jesus Christ. As we have seen, the church represents the kingdom of God. This is the ultimate order, for "the kingdom(s) of the world (must) become the kingdom of our Lord and of his Christ." (Rev. 11:15) This is God's kingdom, and the consummation of it is his to effect in his own time and way. But in the meantime it must be represented by the church which we mold in our time and in our way way. Christ has given us this responsibility. It is we the church who must implement the kingdom of God on earth, and open the door of salvation to all the world! The critical importance of our job is that the kingdom which God eventually establishes will be the kingdom the church makes possible for him to establish! Do we understand this? Do we feel the poignancy of Jesus' question: "Nevertheless, when the Son of Man comes, will he find faith on earth"? (Luke 18:8)

We must first allow Christ to be Lord over us all. United we must challenge the world with Christ's salvation, and we must heal the wounds we have added to his body, so that we may all be one church and the world may believe that it is God who has given Christ to all his human children.